FROM THE LOST LETTERS SENT - BOOK THREE: 1993 - 1994

FROM THE LOST LETTERS SENT - BOOK THREE: 1993 - 1994

Memoirs From An Invisible Songwriter

LORD CHESTER L. BALDWIN II

A Lord Baldwin Happening

Contents

I

AUTHOR'S NOTES

Hello there, **Lord Baldwin** here,... again;

As you are here reading this message I am happy to see your continued interest. So, perhaps you have finished Book ONE and TWO, and are now moving forward to continue finding out what book THREE is all about,... and for those getting ready to continue your experiences with the, *'Lord Baldwin Happening'* (which is; the listening of Lord Baldwin's music as you simultaneously read the Poems, (Lyrics), Memoirs & Notes from this book),... thank you for being here, and for whatever your reasons are, I welcome and thank you for being interested,...

These memoirs and notes and poems began in 1968 where I wrote my first poems (lyrics) at Pemberton Township High School in Burlington County New Jersey, next to the Fort Dix Army Military Installation.

My journey moved west to Portland Oregon where I began writing songs as I learned how to better play guitar. Then I got married, my first daughter, Lori, arrived,...we moved to Washington State,... and over time, I became a father ten time over,... I was called to work with the Scouting program in 1976 and having been a Scout leader registered in the local council ever since,... and a really cool I had the opportunity to be involved with all of my boys as they went through their Scouting days,...

Family,... That word makes my brain reflect on my wife Diane, my 10 children and their significant others and of course, their children,... Wow, looking back at my journey and the directions I went,... I know I made the right choice,... and I am a family man, first and foremost,... And I ended up working various jobs to keep the family going; (you read on and it's all, well maybe mostly all explained to you), I had to learn the varied systems out there, like procedures needed to follow when dealing with the government and bureaucracy, (keep in mind I live in the State Capitol city of Washington State, and the Lacey, Tumwater, Olympia cities ooze with structural orderliness, especially is you want to get on to work with the state,... and like the methods and routines of the schools systems, and maintaining communication with the authorities, the Principals and other administration officials,... what with multiple boys and girls in Black Lake Elementary, Tumwater Junior High and Tumwater High School all at the same time,...

So, as afore mentioned or implied, I had choices to make in my pursuit to shaping my musical career and I decided after the first child was born that that musical career was going to have to take a back seat as I decided that I was going to be that father figure that I never had and be the best dad ever,... And it is my hope that you readers know that my first focus in life was then, and is now, for my wife and kids,...

And so, as far as my musical career was concerned, as you read on you'll find a lot of the frustrations I went through to stop being, 'the Invisible Songwriter' and that maybe someday my work might be recognized and validated,... Yet, the thing is, even though I had real, bonified opportunities to go on the road with my guitar and maybe even conquer the music business in the bargain,... (in the bargain? Does that sound sinister to you?),... From the beginning I made that commitment to myself that I would put my family first, (and that was not and still is not as easy as it sounds),...

So I did the dad thing and worked to fill all the missing parts that were void in my childhood, growing up without a father figure to guide me,... and I hoped to answer some of my kids' questions; questions that went unanswered when I was younger,... questions and answers that might help my own kids to build strong character that they might grow up and become good people,...

Anyway, it came down to me being father first,... and I would work on my music and material along the way,... and along the way might look like after everyone was asleep in the house after eleven at night, and many times on till two in the morning, even though I had to get up by six or seven to go to work,... but in that way, I could take the time to be the best husband and dad that I could possibly be,... Winging it much of the time,...

And along the way I was blessed with a peculiar musical itch,... I was bestowed (blessed) with an artistic perspective and blessed with an awesome gift for comprehending the enchanting magic of music,... And I am thankful for my talents and insights,... and after a while, that awareness, perceptiveness and cognizance was calling to me all the time, wanting to drop whatever I was doing so I might write the intuitions for possible philosophical objectives to some new poetic sketches,... or to learn to play the guitar well enough to sound like and musical chord structures and strategies that were constantly playing in my head,... And along the way I was able to put those words and music to good use,... but it had to be done after everything else,... otherwise, and I did fail at times, but, I was convinced that the family unit would otherwise end up suffering.

This productivity was made possible partially by my taking the mandatory hour-long lunch period to write, every day,... the poetry (lyrics), sometimes writing two a day, but most of the time it would take me the whole hour or even two or three days to get it right,... And to be sure, maybe only one poem out of five was good enough to make the cut,... but that still meant about fifty a year might be considered,...

This here is the **THIRD BOOK** of Lord Baldwin's anthological works; '*From The Lost Letters Sent – Book THREE: 1993 – 1994; (Memoirs From An Invisible Songwriter)*' and From a timeline perspective, this

Book THREE finds Lord Baldwin recording more of his repertoire as well as writing new poetry and creating new musical compositions that he felt impressed to document,... detailing and recording works between July of 1993 and April of 1994,... documenting the lyrics and memoirs of songs, musical compositions and stories from the next ten albums;

21 – That's America For You
22 – One Step Closer, (To The Heart)
23 – Shifted Gears
24 – New Suits
25 – Listening To The News
26 – Work
27 – The New Lover's Waltz
28 – On The Edge Of A Very Strange Light
29 – Dreams For You
30 – City Boy

These ten albums document the **Seventy-Nine** songs that were recorded between July of 1993 and April of 1994,... This productivity was made possible partially by my taking the mandatory hour-long lunch period to write, every day,... the poetry (lyrics), sometimes writing two a day, but most of the time it would take me the whole hour or even two or three days to get it right,... And to be sure, maybe only one poem out of five was good enough to make the cut,... but that still meant about fifty a year might be considered,...

So here we are,... And for you who seek to listen to the albums while you read,... so as to delve a bit deeper and get the arcane connections to some of the thirty-eight albums of the Lord Baldwin's Archive Series,... You are in luck,... It's all out there streaming worldwide,... like twinkling stars in the illusive clouds of cyberspace,... transcending space and time itself and now, it's all around the world,... Again, I thank you for your interest,...

So here we are,... And for you who seek to listen to the albums while you read,... so as to delve a bit deeper and get the arcane connections to some of the thirty-eight albums of the Lord Baldwin's Archive Series,... You are in luck,... It's all out there streaming worldwide,... like twinkling stars in the illusive clouds of cyberspace,... transcending space and time itself and now, it's all around the world,... Again, I thank you for your interest,...

Honesty, I rarely take the time to read what the preface tries to relate, or what is in the introduction, or to delve into the message that the author has presented because I want to just get to the book itself, and instead, knowing my probable audience to be my own family and close friends, this is a chance to let everyone know where my head was at when I started this magnificent journey into the vast domains of music and poetry, coloured by my all-encompassing experiences, good and bad and my particular philosophies of life and love,... all in an effort to help you, the reader, be able to put together a picture of what it was that Lord Baldwin was trying to accomplish,...

Please note as you are about to peruse the contents of this work before you, *'From The Lost Letters Sent - Memoirs Of An Invisible Songwriter - Book THREE: 1993 - 1994'* that it can be broken up into three major parts of interest;

FIRST, *the album Cover Art*, which, as noted previously, I'm delighted with, because I had such fun designing and creating them (as an icon if you will), to represent the songs, the music, the lyrics and poetry of that particular album.

SECOND, *the Words, the Poetry, the Lyrics* – These "*Words For Songs*" come to me in my daily doings, when I'm riding my bike, when I'm trying to go to sleep and sometimes they come to me in my dreams. Sometimes playing my guitar invites the words for songs to come out and play. Sometimes I take an interest in a happening that needed documentation, even if it is just lyrics to a song. Sometimes I am driven by the administering of injustice and inequity to the down-home folks that have to deal with prejudice and discrimination just to live a life here in America, and I am driven to write a poem to reflect the way

I am feeling at that time. I believe in the potential of each song being important, in part from its individual contribution and to its possibilities as a whole especially if it is a concept album. For that sometime in the future.

THIRD, we have the, *"Memoirs From An Invisible Songwriter"* which in and of itself is broken down into two parts;

One; a collection of **stories** that may, or may not relate to the writings of the words for songs, and,...

Two; the **documentations of past happenings**, to give life to and clarity to particular happenings,... and to shed light on projects, explaining my motivations,... and sometimes where I was and what it was that was happening at that time in my life, and then perhaps,... why it was that I felt the need to write the words I did,... and perhaps to explain the challenges, the triumphs and failures, reasonings, and decisions to the song's creation.

When I was originally putting this document together in 2001 as a project I was doing at The Evergreen State College, some of the stories and antidotes, fresh at the time, made a lot of sense so I included most of the documentation created then in hopes of presenting fresh facts (fresh twenty years prior), and to be as true to the moments I was creating things,... Besides being fun diversions to the whole, I believe the stories to be essential to help you gain a more balanced understanding, and it was my hope that some of the stories might shed light on who I was, what I was doing,... and maybe my motivations,... and what it was that shaped me to go in the directions that I did,... and maybe why I did not go in other directions when the opportunities presented themselves. Regrettably, there was always so much more to include, but I needed to keep moving forward to get this work out, and so, what you have here is not complete, nor do I think it ever will be,... and for everything it is not, this documentation is a work in progress,... and I reserve the right to revise, renew, renovate and or add to the **"Memoirs"** and **"Stories"** involved.

As Lord Baldwin's music is now streaming worldwide, this book may act as a companion guide for the listener of Lord Baldwin's material, and for those who might be interested in what thought-processes and insights that Lord Baldwin was going through or was influenced by, along with stories that may be related to the creative processes.

PERHAPS SOME BACKGROUND

House on Margaret Street – Iron Mountain Michigan

In the mid-50s, my family was living in Iron Mountain Michigan where I was influenced early on to what music was all about and listening to the birth of Rock and Roll in my older brother John's bedroom. After my brother David, John's favorite brother, left in 1958, I was delegated to try to fill the gap that David's departure left, and so, while John and I would sit on his bed playing a variety of card games, we would be listening to music on his Westinghouse Tube Radio. From fan magazines of that era, like; **"Teen"** and **"Hep Cats"** and **"Dig"** and

"Rock and Roll Songs" (a few of the titles that John collected along with his "**MAD**" magazines), John was well read and seemed to know everything about the artists that we were listening to, and he loved to share that information, telling me narratives and stories about his favorites; Elvis Presley, Ricky Nelson, Chuck Berry, Bill Haley and the Comets, the Platters, Fats Domino, Gene Vincent, Little Richard, the Diamonds, Pat Boone, the Everly Brothers, the Coasters, Sam Cooke, Jerry Lee Lewis, Tommy Edwards, Conway Twitty, Connie Francis, Jackie Wilson and Buddy Holley. My love for the music only grew even after John went into the navy in 1960.

When John left, he asked me to watch over his stuff while he was gone and he entrusted me with his radio and his magazine collection. I put his radio on the dresser that I shared with my brother Richie and stored John's magazines in a broken wicker hamper in my closet along with my own prized comic books, and then, for safe keeping, I covered the pile with a tattered WWII parachute.

Sadly, maybe six months later, my mother grabbed us kids and ran away (for the second time) from her abusive husband, (we'll just call him; Senior). There was very little time to prepare for the departure and we would be traveling light by Greyhound bus with no space to take wanted possessions; only a change of clothes. I thought that we would be returning after their reconciliation, so I felt all my prized-good stuff was safe. And even years later, knowing the house on Margaret Street had been sold and others were now living there, I felt that I'd be able to go back to that house in Iron Mountain and go into that closet and retrieve all those treasures. That of course, never happened.

Okay, okay, getting off track here. It is obvious that I don't know what to say here or how to say it. Maybe you're asking yourself, why should I care about this book? What is so special about it, and who is this self-proclaimed Lord Baldwin? Well, Lord Baldwin has spent his entire life writing poetry and lyrics and in his later teens began to put music to the words. After composing maybe seventy-five plus songs, from 1966 to 1989, he purchased a **TASCAM 4-track Cassette Recorder** to solidify and document those songs. Not long afterwards, he started recording his songs and then created a number of albums. This book can therefore be used as a companion for and in behalf of, or with the first nine albums that were recorded by Lord Baldwin,...

And now a story,...

In the late spring of 1971, I was accompanying my brother Richie who was driving to "The Pines Resort Hotel" in Fallsburg, New York; located in the Catskills. We were there to go to a concert, arguably I do not remember who it was; I think it was T. Rex ("Bang a Gong (Get It On)") or Emerson, Lake & Palmer. Anyway, not important. We decided to get there early because the seating in those days was FCFS and we wanted to be up front. We arbitrarily arrived two hours early with absolutely no other cars or people there. We went into the facility and found it was totally deserted, but there, up on a short-rise stage, was all the band's instruments and equipment including a "Rickenbacker 325 Rose Morris Fireglo" guitar, kind of like the one John Lennon (the Beatles) and John Fogerty (Credence Clearwater Revival) played. I picked it up from its stand, sat on the edge of the stage and played the three or four chords that I knew. Even with my amateurship and even without it being plugged in, the guitar sang like out and resonated wonderfully. I will admit that the influence of Satan was strong; I was sorely tempted, and in my head I knew that this iconic Rickenbacker 325 Rose Morris Fireglo guitar could very easily be mine. But also, in my head and moreover in my heart, I knew this Rickenbacker guitar was not mine, and that whoever owned this guitar would be very sad to have someone steal it. I said a prayer for strength and after motioning to my brother Richie, I immediately left the building to avoid taking the Rickenbacker guitar. On the drive home the spirit confirmed to me that because of that one small act of honesty and integrity, that I would be blessed to be able to magnify that marvelous musical talent that I knew was inside me, just waiting for me to tap into; waiting to be more fully discovered. It also came to me, that had I taken the Rickenbacker, my musical talents would have been stifled, maybe even taken from me.

I felt a glowing goodness inside me all the way back to our Bungalow at Spanners in Monticello NY, and that good feeling has continued to be with me ever since,...

At the end of the summer of 1971, in Woodstock New York, I bought my first guitar; a **Yamaha 12-string** with a artificial alligator-skin, hard-shell case for two hundred and fifty dollars. I ditched the idea of getting a Guild 12 string (like the one John Denver had on the cover of, "Poems Prayers and Promises"), because, at the time, it was going for around $799.99 which was way beyond my price range. Right after that, with my friends Harvey and Lesa, (and their dog), I went on a road trip across the U.S. to get back to the west coast. Admittedly, I knew nothing about loosening the strings and relieving the tension on the neck and bridge of the guitar, that was packed and sitting up in the back window of the car. Through the corn country of Nebraska and Iowa, the sun, beating directly down on the guitar within the case, ended up cooking and warping the guitar neck. A month later, after newly arriving in Portland Oregon, the Yamaha guitar and the fake alligator hard-shell case was stolen from my apartment; probably (and sadly) by an acquaintance or pseudo friend. I was then down to going to the Portland State University music wing (third floor?) where there was a huge bank of semi-sound-proof piano rooms to practice in, as time would allow.

What happens when that dream that we have been working with for so long, continues to be three or four steps in front of us? What if we can even visualize the dream and see it in motion with others that are moving about, wearing that dream; our dream, meanwhile, that same dream for us continues to be beyond our reach? In spite of all the discouraging voices steeped in negativity, we have to choose to listen to our heart. We must continue to plod on; we are, after all, on a mission.

Never mind the great ones out there on center stage. Never mind the critics that pan your work and criticize your ineptness. And never mind the time it takes to complete that one simple expression of words and music that, arguably pales in the light of the others. We are on a mission; a mission to find our words and our voice and our chord progressions and our vision of what we want others to know us by. We must continue to move forward. and in doing so, knowing that things too easily gained are too little esteemed, we keep chasing that dream, no matter how far in front of us it gets. We can't give up; we refuse to give up. We know that if we want this thing to work, we've got to believe.

And so, as we live and create and do what we feel we must, maybe with the hope that someday we will be noticed and our work, to be validated, we work in a void. A void where we see and hear them but they can't see us. And arguably if and when they do, their dull, arduously obligatory returned look seems to say, "it is so hard for me to tolerate your struggling ineptness." But they come and go quickly and when we get past the nursing of our own broken hearts, we have to know that that recognition can't be our driving motivation, not only because it'll only hurt that much more when it doesn't happen, but as we are living in the new-normal, apathetic world of indifferent people, whose lack of concern for others, or lack of interest in anything that is not self-serving, we have seen the likes of them and we don't want to be one of those guys.

Eventually we look to come to the understanding that in our long and colourful journey, illuminated by the learning-from-our-mistake travels, we are there, in our own world, doing that thing that we love; we are there creating little masterpieces that, if not to anyone else, still has value to us, and to that end, we are kind of living some of the best parts of that dream. And we see what we can do and we know that we have to continue to believe in our dream.

And now it's time for you to find out,... and I hope whomever you are, that you can find enjoyment in these pages of this documentation of these next ten albums along with the corresponding songs,... and that maybe you can find something worthwhile investigating what Lord Baldwin is all about,...

Indubitably Yours,
Lord Baldwin

2

SPECIAL NOTE TO MY FAMILY

I decided that I'd like to say something special, just to you; my children and to my children's children, (my grandchildren), so here goes,... You all know me and know that I love music,... It fills me up with happiness and can help me get out of bad places like when I'm feeling annoyed or angry about something,... Music has healing powers that can mend your soul and repair your broken heart. I want you to know that music can have the same medicinal powers on you too, if you wish.

You may or may not have pondered about this thought, but I want to address this here and now,... There are things in our being that were passed on from generation to generation through our DNA,... things passed on from our mothers and from our fathers that help define the attributes that comprise our physical and chemical makeup,...

New scientific studies now suggest that some of our memories, fears, and behaviors are passed down genetically through generations from our ancestors,... Recent studies done by epigenetic scientists and researchers even suggest that we receive loads of genetic memories from our parents, grandparents, and further ancestors, in an instinctive effort by their DNA to better prepare ours for difficult experiences that they have faced, such as fear, disease, or trauma,... These epigenetic scientists also study how genes are inherited and the changes to those genetics that we exhibit, even when those changes are not essential to our DNA,... These changes can be affected or recalled by our experiences, age, environment, and health.

It came to me one night a couple of months ago that within this receiving of coded genetic DNA that we were all given, through the transferal of genes from our fathers, mothers, grandmothers, grandfathers, etc., we also received special gifts and talents that we, if we so discover, could use and magnify,... Let me be even more plain on this; our Heavenly Father has instilled within us, many gifts and talents, expecting us to discover them and to magnify those talents to accomplish great things while here on this earth.

I believe that examining our heritage can help us to identify some of those gifts and talents,... I don't have too much documentation to extrapolate data from the past because I only vaguely knew my great grandmother Viola Snook, on my mother's side, who, played harmonica in her teens in a band in 1885 and continued playing her whole life till her passing in 1970, but I can say with a certainty that both my grandparents on my mother's side, my mother, who played piano and early on transposed musical documents for my father, father, who played accordion, organ and piano professionally in the early 50s,... and they all inherited and used their special gift of music that were passed down to them,...

Some of **our** ancestors, like my mother and father, knew that they had this gift of music and they shared it with the world as they went about their lives doing what they did,... some of our other ancestors got busy with life and maybe magnified other talents that they recognized early on,... It doesn't mean they didn't have the gift of music, it just meant that that particular gift might not have been discovered or might not have been as important to them as other pursuits,...

Okay, so where am I going with this,... I came to the realization that not long after discovering that I had these special talents and the gift of music, I began to move quickly forward in my understanding of how chord progressions worked, and it all seemed to happen logically in my head,... There is no substitute for **practice**,... but I found that as I was practicing, the tediousness and redundancies did not bother me at all and I found a kind of joy in my eventual progress,...

I had wanted to be a singer/songwriter for a long time, but there was something in my DNA that told me, 'of course you can do that — you and your ancestorial line were instilled with musical talents from our Heavenly Father *many* generations ago with the gift of music' and therefore, you were born with the gift of music,... and how cool is that?

Long story short, you, my children and grandchildren also inherited my DNA which means that you too have these special talents and the gift of music,...

IF YOU WISH, you only need to search for and discover them within, to magnify your powers,... I say, *if you wish*, because not everyone, even those blessed with these talents will feel the need or want to amplify the music powers within,... There is a price to pay for becoming a musician,... beyond your special gifts, as with everything in life, and for even the most gifted of artists and writers, as mentioned before, there is a basic prerequisite and necessity for you to **practice**, and practice and practice even more to get to a higher level of proficiency,...

Still, it is your choice to go in that direction or not, but please know this; not everyone has the special talents and the gift of music like you do,... and unless you hate music and everything about it, which I'm pretty sure is not happening in your DNA, it costs you nothing but your time and effort to explore this fascinating world of music.

One more thing; your talent, that music gift we're talking about is powerful and very much like magic. It should not be used inappropriately. You should not use your powers to hurt others or to puff yourself up and be full of yourself, or to gain advantage at someone else's expense, or to hurt someone that is less talented than you. It doesn't mean you can't be competitive at times or that after you've reached a level of proficiency that you can't go out and make money with your talents. There are many good people in this world that use their musical powers to pay their rent and to buy food. That is okay. You need to value your musical powers and know that if you want the powers to stay, if you want your musical talents to grow, you will need to do it in the spirit of kindness and love and you need to be good.

Now, look inside your being and find your powers and magnify your talents, whether they be music or writing or art or something else,... Those talents are all there, you just have to find them and use them wisely. Please know that I love, EACH AND EVERY ONE OF YOU, and wish you happy hunting in finding and *using* your true talents,....

3

– 21 – THAT'S AMERICA FOR YOU – 1993 –

4

NOTES ABOUT THE COVERS

Note On The New Cover: So, I took the essence of the statue of Liberty put a set of clouds that had relatively the same lighting source; coming from above and to the front of the statue. Then added some extra fluffy, whiter, (less gray) clouds in front of the ominous ones to give the picture a sense of home amongst the turmoil.

Notes On The Original Covers:

I liked the Statue of Liberty and it was my first go-to image to reflect America, but I had no idea where this first picture came from so it had to go.

Also, the back cover was also full of people I didn't know so I couldn't use it either.

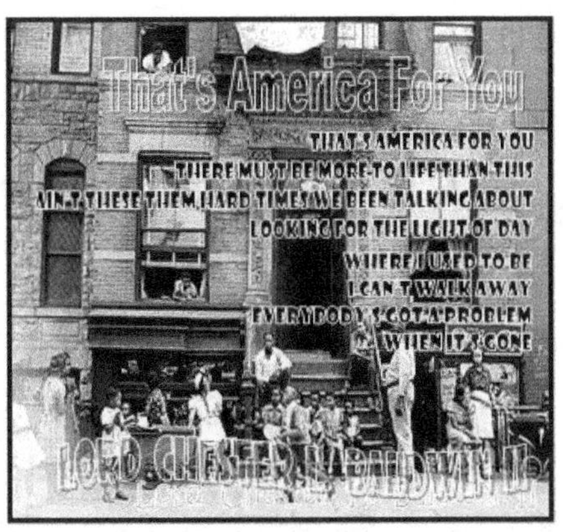

5

THAT'S AMERICA
FOR YOU

That's America For You
There Must Be More To Life Than This
Ain't These Them Hard Times
(We Been Talking About)
Waiting For The Lights To Change
Where I Used To Be
I Can't Walk Away
Everybody's Got A Problem
When It's Gone

6

That's America For You

They're working four tens and setting their own trends
to take a three-day weekend at the coast.
Though it's a struggle to get there, it's a family affair
and they all work for the goals they strive for most.
There's always something around
that tries to break things down
but they deal with the conflicts as they arrive.
And so they follow their star in an old Buick car
heading out somewhere down interstate five.

That's America for you
—you can go your own way.
That's America for you
—living in the U.S.A.

There's folks in every part with convictions in their heart,
standing by their commitments to do the best.
Daily battles fought and won as they get that job done,
dedicated to the pursuit of happiness.
There's some people who'd say

we ain't worth what we get paid,
as they sneak around behind the back porch.
Possessive of our game and wishing they had the same
they can only emulate and follow our torch.

Hey you know, that's America for you
—you can go your own way.
That's America for you
—living in that U.S.A.

There is no other shore that a foreigner can go
and feel accepted from far and wide.
There is no other place made up of such diverse race
and yet in contrast can coexist side by side.
As individuals or teams,
they can follow out their dreams
ideologically whichever way they see.
Where else but in this land can a person take their stand
and be anything, become whatever they want to be.

Hey, that's America for you
—you can go your own way.
That's America for you
—living in the U.S.A.
Doesn't get much better than this, Babe.

7

There Must Be More To Life Than This

Working the convenience store from midnight to dawn,
sleeping off the day
till the next shift is on.
He's been there for three years with no hope of change,
his family relationships
are spinning down the drain.

Five-forty in the morning, the sun begins to rise,
stares out a little window,
dreaming of some other time.
He can't remember why he compromised to take this shift,
but thinks that there must be more to life than this.

Quitting school for big money was hard to avoid,
then the layoff after summer
and now she's unemployed.
Some bridges she burned on the way
when things were looking good,

are needed now for crossing back
but she's unsure if she could.
Bills keep coming in as she tries to organize
her contemplative thoughts
and the facts from all the lies.
She knows what they all think, she's on so many lists,
but she knows that there must be more to life than this.

Somewhere out in the middle of Nowhere, U.S.A.,
staring into space
wondering how to get away,
I've justified the past, put the family all to bed,
as my future is still waiting
for the answers to be said.
I can see within the fabric of my life singing this song,
I've taken a wrong turn
and can't admit that I was wrong.
Not sure what I should do, remorseful of what I've missed,
I feel that there must have to be more to life than this.
More to life than this.
More to life;
More,...

8

Ain't These Them Hard Times, (We Been Talking About)

Richie been looking all over the northwest
for work to keep his family out of debt.
Turned down, patronized and strung out like the rest;
not too many paying jobs to get.
Bad back, complications, Ray's stuck in the mire,
down to picking up river debris.
Take it home, chop it up, throw it on the fire,
one short step away from poverty.

Ain't these them hard times we been talking about
supposed to come some future year?
Better board up the windows and load up the guns,
because hard times are finally here.

Standing in a food line with a rock churning in my gut,
for the government cheese that's passed around.

Dignity and pride are eating at me but,
man's gotta do something when he's down.
Taxes due, the payments late and the bank at the door,
the car's been repossessed and towed away.
Have to sell what I can and I hope they don't ask for more,
I'm just barely getting by from day to day.

Ain't these them hard times we been talking about
supposed to come some future year?
Better board up the windows and load up the guns,
because hard times are finally here.
Seems like pretty soon, we're all heading for the war
over shelter, fuel and enough to eat.
Can't hardly trust the neighbors anymore,
just the true friends and our family down the street.

Ain't these them hard times we been talking about
supposed to come some future year?
Better board up the windows and load up the guns,
hard times are finally here.

9

Waiting For The Lights To Change

Waiting, preaching what I know from where I've been,
and here I sit as life runs away.
Searching, reaching, yet I'm still, in between
looking to answer the questions I pray.

Sitting in traffic, staring at the red light,
thinking how life runs things so strange.
It seems so tragic, cars in front and cars behind,
all waiting for that light to change.

Ain't we all waiting for the light to change.
Ain't we all looking for the light of day.

No difference from college, just climbing the ropes
to search the soul's philosophy.
I just want the knowledge; assurance that my hopes
have substance more than some silly dream.

Waiting too long, for the day to arrive,
but here I remain in constant delay.
Nighttime is so long, as I can't seem to revive
from dreams and nightmares left to my fate.

Ain't we all looking for the light of day.
Ain't we all waiting for the lights to change.

It's taking to long, and I want to break away,
but here I am, blocked in and I have to stay.

Ain't we all waiting for the lights to change.
Ain't we all looking for the light of day.

IO

Where I Used To Be

We've all worked hard to receive our day,
many haven't reached yet but are well on the way.
And as I have saved time that I might find my due,
I've climbed a lot of mountains but I've fallen down a few.
The past; I have used away but now it's coming back to me,
I have come a long hard way to end up where I used to be.
I'd like to think it was right to strive for,
but after what happened, I'm not sure anymore.
The years I spent working to grow strong and tall,
to throw it all away for no reason at all.
For all I have done to now, to gain what it is I seek,
I have come a long hard way to end up where I used to be.
It's a give and take; it's use or save.
People work hard to get to their own early graves,
Or slowly but surely find the job they can do less
but I'm starting all over and I'm in such a mess.
I see my future road, and it's a path I've know and seem.
I have come a long hard way just to end up
where I used to be; where I used to be.

I Can't Walk Away

Temperatures rise and anger fills the void.
Trying not to confront
there's no way to avoid.
Wishing for an out but none can be found,
knowing there's no choice,
but to stand my ground.
Anger leads to this showdown; who knows what for,
but there's no way to leave
with dignity anymore.
I can only stand and fight, there's no other way,
I may win or lose
but I can't walk away.

Who knows how these things ever get this far?
All I know is I'm stuck
with the way they are.
To fight for nothing is the idiocy of this town.
I can't compromise
and I can't back down.
Too late for talking, only one thing left to do,

I got to get tough
and see this thing through.
With everybody here; there's nothing left to say,
I'll give it my best shot,
but I can't walk away.

Do parents just forget how things were years ago?
Well, there isn't any difference
from all I know.
To turn and run away is worse than just to lose,
for the pride and dignity
can also cut or bruise.
There is no retreat with honor anymore;
it's stay and fight the battle,
no matter what for.
Determination set, I don't want to stay,
but now I got no choice,
and I can't walk away.
No, I give it my best shot,
but I can't walk away.
I may win or lose
but I can't walk away.

12

Everybody Has A Problem

Everybody's got a problem,
everybody knows how to sing the blues at times
when things fall to doubt, while being brought down,
when you live in a drought,
you do without.

Everybody's got a reason,
right or wrong, the time for action is now.
But the questions bite deep, and the wounded won't keep,
the answers are asleep
hidden in a garbage heap; hidden in a garbage heap.

Everybody's got solutions,
ways to improve all the injustices of these times.
To shine and shed light, in the darkness of night.
Being wise with insight
but they won't get the right;
they never get the right.

13

When It's Gone

The children are so special, they're a part of us.
Wild with wonder, excitement and the thrill of it.
But they're babes today and teens tomorrow;
then they're off to the war.

And when they're gone, you've got to live on.
Carve a piece of every dawn; you've got to live on.
They say that everything has a beginning;
a time for being and a time for dying.
It's all just a here today world, gone tomorrow;
hardly had time to enjoy,

oh, but when it's gone, you've got to live on.
Carve a piece of every dawn; you've got to live on.
The old folks of your past are locked in cages;
Still shining from the wisdom of the ages.
But they start to slow down so you lock them away
so they won't be under your feet.
And when they're gone, you've got to live on.
Carve a piece of every dawn, you've got to live on.

14

MEMOIRS & NOTES - 21 -
'THAT'S AMERICA FOR YOU'

That's America For You

(1993) – in 1992, Koichi Kato, a top Japanese politician said that while individual politicians had their own views, he publicly characterized all working men and women in America and the U.S. Work Force, Lazy. It was because

of him that I wrote this poem. I was over at one of my neighbor's houses, I don't remember why I was there, but the subject came around about his job, and he related to me his feelings. I never asked but was told how he worked hard in an environment that was hostile and sometimes dangerous. Yet his words come back to me like it was yesterday, and he said, "they may not appreciate what I do and I may not like everything I'm doing there, but I will do the best job I can." And it was from his attitude contrasting the negativity of Koichi Kato that I tried to document a little bit of what I feel America and is working people are all about.

Side Note:

I really hoped to make this album something totally different from my past albums and I kind of hoped for an upbeat and positive representation, and even after I recorded the album, I thought that I was accomplishing that end, but after a year of listening to this album I'm not so sure that its original album conception was achieved. Still, it remains to be one of my favorites and I listen to it all the time.

There Must Be More To Life Than This

(1993) – Written in 1993, this song documents real people in real life situations; people that I had encountered just prior to writing this poem. I met the first character early one morning as I stopped at an AM-PM Arco gas station to get gas, sometime around six. He was working at this gas station convenience store, doing the graveyard shift, earning minimum wage. He related to me a few of his philosophical ideas and told me that he was concerned that he was working all night by himself, and he was worried about getting shot by someone that was robbing the place, late at night or in the early morning. As I was getting a small bag of chips to subsidize my lunch, I caught him gazing out the window, seemingly wondering if there might be more to his existence than what he was doing at that time. When he turned back to me to take my money, his eyes seemed to ask me for acceptance of him and his circumstances. I smiled amiably and wished him a good day.

I was at the college in the computer lab and helping a woman format her Writing 101 document and we got to talking, (see side note below). She was getting close to graduating from the community college but she had recently found herself compromising her own planned directions in her life, and then settling; just settling for the money and the job itself. After she had given all of herself to this company for a length of time, they just let her go. As I was sitting there, listening to her story, I was thinking of how many others are lured away from their own heart's direct, only to find themselves betrayed. While she was talking to me, I felt that she wanted me to accept her and not judge her for her apparent compromise. I let her know that, in many ways, I was no different than her. Certainly, I have spent many years not lost, but distracted and energies diverted career wise, but though I was a bit unhappy with my present circumstances, I needed to provide for my family. Even though by this time in my life I was enjoying what it was that I was doing, still there were other things there that continued to consume me and my energies which I thought could possibly be better served in some other capacity. When she left the computer lab with a lighter step, I felt like she had come to some agreement with herself and that she would do well to finish her education and then, take the next step.

Side Note:

Over the years it has become apparent to me, and Diane has commented on this more than once; maybe there's something in my personality or demeanor, my simple manner, maybe my non-threatening appearance, a trustful but unassuming face, maybe it's my easy-going disposition and nature, whatever it is, I seem to have this thing where people seem to not only trust me, but moreover, they feel comfortable enough to want to talk to me and tell me their life stories. I think it's because they sense that I will listen to them; and after all, we all want to be heard.

Ain't These Them Hard Times (We've Been Talking About)

(1985) – It was right after I wrote this song that I was coined as a doomsday prophesier by my own brother Ray, even though it inspired him to write a song called, "*Soon The Snow Will Fall In July,*" which was played equally when we got together. This song truly documents some of the more trying times that us Baldwins were going through in the '80s. It documents Richard's unemployment problems, Ray's health problems and dealing with others' perceptions while he and his children are down on my dad's farm picking up pieces of wood to keep his house heated. And then there's my real-life experience in Thurston County, and the degradation of standing in this long line outside a church in downtown Olympia with many of the other misfortunates, waiting for their opportunity to be handed a brick or two of government cheese.

That same cheese had become an important topic for the press in the

1980s, when they learned about milk products that were being stored across the nation, while millions of Americans, (like myself) were on the poverty spectrum and feeling a sense of food insecurity. During that same time, President Ronald Reagan's administration cut the budget on the US federal food stamp program which Ray was in desperate need. On December 22, 1981, Reagan signed and authorized into law that five hundred and sixty million pounds (250,000 metric tons) of cheese that the government, (the Commodity Credit Corporation (CCC)) had been stockpiled, should and would be released.

It was difficult to get the cheese; it being administered in the middle of a work day. Diane did not want to go down there, and arguably it would have been a hardship for her to have to stand out there in the cold in that long line, trying to keep Meridith, 3, and Ben, 1, from embarrassing her, and also, her being pregnant with Stephen. Still, I knew it would subsidize our meager circumstances, so it was up to me to go there every month, hoping I could get through the long line during my lunch hour or try to slip in and out of there as fast as possible. Whether it was my stifled dignity or my self-esteem issues, I too was reluctant, humiliated, and at first, I was just kind of ashamed to be standing there in that line; because at that moment, it made me one of them. I wasn't making much money at the time and I knew we could use the cheese, and that the cheese could help our food budget. So I swallowed that pride and accepted myself to be with my newly associated friendships of the financially poor brothers and sisters. After a couple of months, the task got easier. People started recognizing me there and likewise I started seeing a lot of the regulars, who, knowing I had to get back to work, would sometimes even give me cuts in line, and I was more comfortable being a part of the other insignificants and them with me. The processed cheese did come in real handy at times, and because there was other organizations involved, there was often other foods; ripe or over-ripe produce, and other passed pull date items like bread given away. Sometimes I would leave there with a good-sized box full of food items. Besides the occasional moldy bread or over-ripe produce, we never let any of the food that they gave me go to waste, and Diane and I were grateful for what we received.

My reference to taxes and bank and repossession of cars was a cumulative of experiences I had with Ray and Richie. In the decadent, self-indulgent era of the 80s, we were all scraping bottom, living the life of the less fortunate, though arguably, being white privileged, we were not faced with some of the demoralizing and degrading problems faced by people of color.

Richie had his car repossessed and towed away because he was out of work and money. I was unemployed for a time in 1985 and went down to Ray's house in Canby Oregon in hopes of doing some side work. I was sleeping on the couch at Ray's house one morning when there came a persistent to the point of annoying knock on Ray's door. When I went to the door, a well-dressed man in a suit stood there looking at me like I was a degenerate. I told him that I was not Ray, and that Ray had already left that morning. After I made it clear that I was Ray's brother and not Ray, the man curtly explained that he had come over a few times before and that he was looking for some considerable interaction with Ray. I reiterated that Ray wasn't home and the man angrily all but called me a liar. He walked around the front of the house trying to look inside the windows. This angered me and I told him that I didn't like his inference that I wasn't telling the truth and I told him that I thought he needed to leave. He looked at me real close to see how serious I was, and I looked back at him with strong determination, like I was going to take his head off, he apologized and with a little more regard, told me that Ray hadn't made a payment for three months on a set of encyclopedias that he'd bought, and he said that he either wanted the money owed or he would take the encyclopedias back. To avoid any more confrontation, the man took out his business card, wrote a note on the back, then he opened up the mailbox and put his business card in it, and without any apologies or farewell, he quickly walked out to the curb, got in a car and drove away. When Ray got back from Oregon City I related the story to him. He laughed, got the card out of the mailbox, read the back and then threw it into his fireplace.

Waiting For The lights To Change

(1992) – Like many people in a "needing" situation, I too was searching for that pie in the sky. It dawned on me one day that, as I was feeling sorry for myself, pondering my choices, entrenched in all the trappings of what I believed to be my pathetic circumstances, I came to the realization that, in a way, it really didn't matter how bad my circumstances were, there was always that someone else worse off than me, and I thought to myself how everybody is looking for that wonderful moment when everything will change their lives and justify all the hassle and harassment from others, all the degradation I've been going through and all the self-deprivation I needed to sacrifice to get my family from here to there.

Side Note:

Ain't we all waiting for the lights to change? Haven't we all been in a situation at work or in our dreams where we're in some holding pattern, waiting for the situation to change or for permission or approval to move forward, or for our financial situation to change enough to get to the next level, or to receive the whatever or whereabouts to move forward to get closer to accomplishing that illusive, or whatever it is we feel would make our jobs and or our lives better? And ain't we all waiting for the lights to change?

Another Side Note:

Ain't we all looking for the light of day? So we're going through this thing; doesn't matter specifically what it is, but we're getting that thing done, it may be a small accomplishment or it may be a long-range goal, it may be to get something done or it may be we need something that will fix the hole where the rain gets in, but ultimately I believe that we all continue to do things, sometimes not easy things, with that certain goal in mind, and whether that benefit goal is to shore up our loving family or to reach exaltation, ain't we all looking for the prize at the end of our illusory rainbow? And ain't we all looking for the light of day?

Where I Used To Be

(1980) – I began working at JW Electronics in 1974. In 1978 I left to work for a division of Georgia Pacific; a cardboard factory, but after a host of odd things happening like me breaking my leg or getting laid off for a month, I went back to school and then eventually crawled back to work at JW Electronics. When I returned to JW Electronics I started over as a driver-deliverer of parts, making a little bit more money than before, but not that much more. In 1982 I was let go, mostly due to a difference of opinion (and arguably attitude) with my brother-in-law Jack. I then worked for three years in the funeral business at Forest Funeral Home, but towards the end of 1985 the funeral home was bought up by another funeral home that would manage both facilities with one staff, and so, I was once again out of the job. I did a few odd things for a couple of months, collected unemployment and ultimately returned back to JW Electronics. When I returned, I was again, a driver-deliverer of electronic parts. I then worked my way up the ladder to an order picker, then I working on the front counter again answering phones and taking orders, all the time wanting to be an outside salesman for the money and the prestige. That never happened though, and JW Electronics went out of business in 1990. The ironic thing about this song is that when I came back to JW Electronics the first time I wrote this song and it prophetically heralded in two more times and this song was as true each time.

Side Note:

I did realize that sometimes to get through life with commitments and responsibilities, I would find that the cost might end up being the loss of my own forward progress. I make it a habit to sing my songs to my kids, maybe not so much now, especially because I'm so busy going to school in the evenings or to scouts or sometimes work, but all of my children will remember me for those moments while they were laying in their beds listening to me, as I sat on the floor in the hallway be-tween the bedrooms, singing to them. And each one of my children has their own favorites that, when I pulled my guitar out, they would shout

out their requests. This song is one of Lori's favorites and she always asks for it.

I Can't Walk Away

(1991) – I seem to vacillate over being either a nonviolent pacifist hippie, or a radical that questions authority with anger, like a rebel without cause. I think we all have our own moods and when I wrote this song, I was reminded of the moments when I was faced with a defining moment of fight or flight, that is, whether to stand and face the adversary or to run to a place of safety. Sometimes the rule is, stand and face the adversary.

Having moved around from Portland to California to Oregon to Alaska to Iron Mountain to Portland to California to Oregon to California to New Jersey to New York to New Jersey to Oregon, and having gone to 13 different schools, there were many "new kid in town" moments in my life where I had to establish boundaries while proving myself, (sometimes, ending up in a fight), and other moments where I was put into the compromising position, if for no other reason than, my unsightly acne face or maybe my passive disposition, or someone needed to prove to their friends that I was to be taught who was the boss, where I would be either branded as a coward that runs away or someone that would have to stand and fight. Yes, there were impossible odds at times where I knew going in that I would probably get beat up anyway, but I stayed. I always had to stay. And sometimes I got pounded on and sometimes I won the battle.

What I hoped to capture with this song was the apprehension and anxiety, the viewpoint, however positive or negative, the insubordinate defiance and attitude needed to go into the mindset of a fight, and hopefully, the senselessness of the selection process young boys and girls have to go through, and I hoped to capture a bit of the reality of the way it all was.

Side Note:

There is a different mindset between someone taking the aggressive, offensive stance, like my big brother Ray

who to me, seemed to need to prove on a daily basis that he was a tough guy,... and he was a tough guy,... because he was always shorter in statute, Ray learned early on that if he didn't want to be constantly picked on, he would have to fight back,... and fight back he did, taking on anyone that tried to mess with him regardless of size or age,... and over time, as a safety factor, Ray took an aggressive stance with everyone he interacted with,... and by the time Ray was a Freshman at North Marion High School, everybody knew that Ray had a very short fuse,... and nobody, not even any of the Seniors messed with him,...

My Brother Ray at North Marion High School - 1965

But there is a different mindset between someone taking the aggressive stance or someone taking the defensive position,... where choices are simply to run or stand and fight. Motivations are different too; my motive in defending myself was almost always to preserve my status quo; to shield myself from the offender, to get out with the least amount of hostility,... and then, perhaps secondarily, in hopes of preserving my dignity and bolster my supposed image, I would want to do what I could to insure that this confrontation only happens once.

This last part is most important because bullies like repeat business, especially ones that they know, fear them. If it happened that I was going down in the fight, and there were many times that I did, I would still want to go down fighting; bullies do not like victims that strike back and especially with vengeful fury, and over all the playground scrimmages I experienced, and the many, after-school choose-offs, because I fought back with veracity, except for the gang-bully episodes where two or more were beating me up, there was never a second time.

Bullies also know that, aside from looking bad as the victim shows no fear and fights back, it might also expose vulnerabilities, and

when their victim aggressively fights back there is a good chance the bully is going to get hurt and that is not part of the mindset of the bully, but even worse is the possibility that they bit off more than they could chew and that after they'd taken a beating, they were going to lose the battle in the end,... and that would not be good for their reputations, and bullies are all about reputation to entice fear in others,...

But I also knew the other side of my brother Ray as a man searching for a better life for himself and his kids,... and a person with honest principles and worthwhile beliefs that, because of his adversities, carried the weight of a lot of problems on his shoulders,... problems that he faced head-on, taking on his hardships sometimes, harsh financial conditions with a vengeance and determination,...

Everybody Has A Problem

(1973) – Diane and I moved from a very nice apartment in downtown Portland Oregon called the Estelle Apartments to a place, across the river and up Hawthorne Street about 17 blocks into a place we called the Chinese Castle, not only because it was owned by a tiny Chinese woman and her two sons, but also because it was kind of shaped like a pagoda and it was painted bright yellow with orange-red trim.

There is a lot of stress moving from one place to the next, only to be complicated by the fact that, and at any moment, Diane was ready to have our first baby, Lori. So it was late November, I was carrying all the stuff in and up the narrow stairway to the second floor duplex apartment. The stairs took a right angle halfway up, and as I was resting on that landing, Diane said something from up within one of the rooms above. I don't even remember what it was that she said or implied, but whatever it was, it was taken wrongly, and for the rest of that day I was not communicating well. After I finished moving our stuff in, I sat on the stairs and wrote the words and music to this song. In a way, it took on a whole different meaning than what I had intended, so I changed a few things around, and although the song no longer reflected anger but rather the commonality of how we have problems, reasons for out actions and possible solutions, (albeit what we think at the time to be for our own resolution and maybe not having the other's best interests in mind), I think that the song turned out to be a good thing and has endured since 1973.

Side Note:

Before we got married, I lost my job as Night Manager at Burger Chef. From today's standard it would never happen today, but back then,... But here's what happened, the General Manager, Mr. Ricketts was promoted to Regional Manager and so he took his family and moved to Indianapolis. He was replaced by a woman named Twana who transferred in from a store in Seattle. As Twana arrived, she brought with her, seven girls that had worked for her in her Seattle store. Within a week she let all the male workers go except me. She also fired most of the other girls that I had worked with for years. After she saw how things were done in the Portland store, and when she was comfortable, I got my walking papers too. When I filed for unemployment insurance I was denied because the unemployment office was told by Twana that I had quit. With one of the unemployment office supervisors there, we called Twana and the unemployment office supervisor asked, "Did you fire Mr. Baldwin?"

"No." Twana replied "I did not."

The unemployment office supervisor looked at me suspiciously and asked, "Did Mr. Baldwin do something wrong to cause his dismissal?"

Twana replied, No."

The supervisor looked puzzled. "So," the supervisor continued, "would you hire him back then?"

Twana replied, "no, I don't want to have any males working for me. I only want females."

The supervisor's eyes grew large as she continued, "So," the supervisor pressed, "Do I understand you right when you said that you let Mr. Baldwin go because of his gender?"

"Yes." Twana calmly replied.

The supervisor turned to me with a questioning scowl and said firmly, "So you fired him?"

"No," Twana insisted, "I just let him go."

"Well Twana," the supervisor retorted, "Your letting Mr. Baldwin go under such conditions is constituted by the federal government as the same as you firing him."

"No it's not." Twana replied heatedly.

"Well yes it is." The supervisor replied, turning to me with a smile, "And I'm afraid you will be contributing to his unemployment insurance."

Another Side Note:

We got a TV after we arrived In Iron Mountain, 1956-57. It was situated in the living room on the main floor of the house. I was fascinated by it and would get up early to watch whatever was on at the time. I loved the Max Fleischer cartoons, like Betty Boop, Superman, Koko the Clown and Popeye, as well as Warner Brothers cartoons from the 30s like Bosco and Porky Pig, and the 40s like Bugs Bunny and Daffy Duck. Although they did not play Disney, there were many other cartoons from less known studios like, Tom and Jerry, Heckle and Jeckle, Woody Woodpecker and Mighty Mouse. When I got back from school, I would watch the TV till just before Senior got home from work, so as to avoid interacting with him. He would ofttimes come home in a bad mood, and was unpredictable at best.

After the second BIG HURT, and with David gone, I stopped watching the TV. I spent a lot of my free time outside and clear of Senior. When I was downstairs, I avoided any contact with Senior and when I found myself seemingly trapped down there, and had to find a way to get past him, I would animate my movements and pretend that I needed to go to the bathroom really bad and then I would run upstairs. I started feeling insecure, and I was scared to be in the same room with Senior. That scene of David and Senior coming up the stairs haunted me for a long time. And after a few times of getting angry looks from Senior, I began to fear that I would be next in line for Senior to take his wrath out on. Afterall, John was working with him at the gas station and Richie was, well, Richie had the gift of charm so he was in no danger. Mother must have known because I was seeing more of her upstairs than ever before. I think the thing I missed the most was feeling free to come and go in that family household. The loss of freedom and weary feeling of being constrained in the second-floor domain and not being able to watch cartoons or the Mickey Mouse show again.

When It's Gone

(1972) – Although I was not a parent at the time that I wrote this song, I was acutely aware of some of the special qualities that many children possessed, and the fact that they were constantly and quickly growing from whatever stage they were in, I would either watch them as they gradually transformed in to something else and maybe not even notice the changes , or I would see them months or maybe years later and readily notice the changes that occurred in size, attitude, and demeanor. I thought about the fact that recognizing the value and fragile perspectives of some of the temporary things we encounter in life was a plus; we are all watchers as well as being watched by other watchers and as life comes and goes, we see the progress and the parade, and when the parade has passed, we go home. But at the same time, someone is watching us and we are their parade and we will pass and they will go home. It seemed to me that one of the most important things that we can do while we are still alive and part of someone else's parade, is to try and grasp what ever piece of life that is put before us and do whatever we can with it.

Side Note:

In my grandmother's home it was expected that when someone in the family got old, the family would take care of them; period. When Grandma Snook got to be 90, her daughter Leda (my grandma Scarbrough), and her daughter Evelyn (my great Aunt), were going to move Grandma Snook in with Aunt Evelyn's place,

Grandma & Grandpa Snook

but Grandma Snook didn't want that and instead, Grandma Snook moved into an apartment (about a half a mile from grandma's house); it was small and simple enough so that Grandma Snook could continue and manage for herself. Grandma Scarbrough was there almost every day, (and Aunt Evelyn was over there mostly on the weekends), to make sure that Grandma Snook had everything she needed or even at times, wanted. Grandma Scarbrough would bring dinners and canned fruits and vegetables, bread, cookies, whatever she felt Grandma Snook might need. And there was a time when Grandma Snook got ill and ended up in Grandma Scarbrough's place or Aunt Evelyn's place until Grandma Snook got better. So it was, and that kind of care continued for years until Grandma Scarbrough passed away in 1973.

I was maybe 13 when my mother, my brothers, Richie and Charlie, my sister Mary and I all ended up in Portland Oregon after taking a succession of buses from Iron Mountain Michigan. As always, we landed at Grandma Scarbrough's home. (Grandma Scarbrough's place was where my mother would go when things got too out of hand with Senior, (who was abusive with mother, and when drunk, could get physically dangerous). After we arrived in Portland, mother hid Richie and I over at Grandma Snook's apartment, fearing that my dad might want to kidnap us. We stayed there a couple of weeks until mother finally called my dad and found out that he had no interest in kidnapping us and rock the delicate boat of a marriage he was experiencing with his wife, Inez. Sorry, I'm getting too far away from this side note; my point was, is that, I discovered while living with my 96-year-old grandmother that there was this, "wisdom of the ages" inside her, anxiously waiting and desperately wanting to be shared with someone that would take the time to listen.

A year later we were back with Senior, (another story for another time), in California, living in the Belle Acres trailer park. Across the street, there was a convalescence home that, I would get curious about, and I would find myself over there visiting the folks inside. Again, it was full of men and women that were starved for the attention of anyone who would give it to them. Each with their treasure full of stories that needed to be shared. I have never forgotten those folks there and to this day, I take my guitar to their facilities to plat, or as a Boy Scout leader, would take a group of boys, and barring from them laying havoc to the place, we would visit with the folks there.

Another Side Note:

Both my brothers John and David were in the armed forces and during the Vietnam War Era, although John was the only one that went there in 1964 to 1968. It seemed a shame that John would graduate from high school and join the navy and then the Air Force to somehow end up on the front line of what was to be a war that we couldn't win.

Heroes and villains,... John was proud to be in the Air Force and he was totally flabbergasted when he heard about how some U.S. Army men of the Charlie Patrol led by Lt. William Calley had covered up the carnage for a year after it was reported in the Amer-

Nixon And The My Lai Massacre Coverup

ican press,...John was outraged as was the world,... that brutality of the killings and the official cover-up fueled anti-war sentiment and further divided the United States over the Vietnam War,... After Hugh C. Thompson, Jr. a helicopter pilot, who was flying a reconnaissance mission,... somehow stopped the My Lai Massacre,... Heroes and villains,... Afterwards, Lt. William Calley was charged with six counts of premeditated murder in the death of 109 Vietnamese civilians at My Lai in March 1968,... Lt. William Calley was tried and convicted to life in prison,... President Nixon reduced Calley's sentence to a light punishment—three years of house arrest,... Heroes and villains,...

15

❦

- 22 - ONE STEP CLOSER
TO THE HEART - 1993

16

NOTES ABOUT THE COVERS

Notes On The New Cover:

As you can see, except for my name change, I used the exact same cover again, maybe because I created the first one years ago; no copywrite infringement. Thing is, it was hard to get the lettering just right and the graphics symmetrical,... Plus, I loved the two doves that the cherub is looking after.

Notes On The Original Covers:

I used the exact cover for the front

and this lovely picture of a lady holding her baby for the back cover. The baby looking like he or she is anxious to nurse.

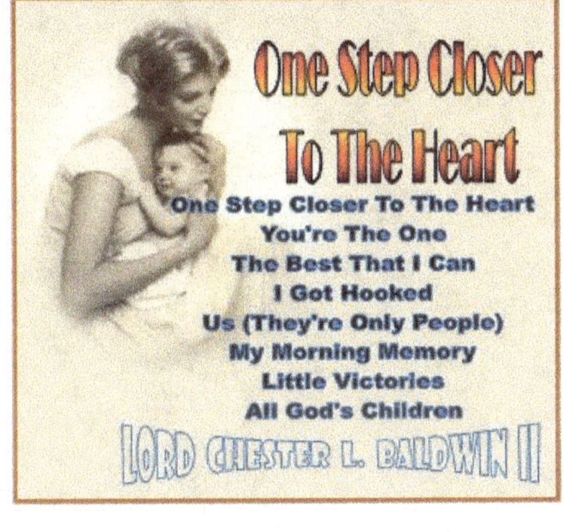

17

ONE STEP CLOSER TO THE HEART

One Step Closer To The Heart
You're The One
The Best That I Can
I Got Hooked
Us (They're Only People)
My Morning Memory
Little Victories
All God's Children

18

One Step Closer To The Heart

Over and over we wait; either too early or too late,
as spectators wager the fate of our rise and fall.
Confused by signs all around,
dictating this love we've found,
and in mediocrity we're bound to lose it all.
Detours and roadblocks are slowing us down
preventing the wonderful start,
oh, but we're moving one step closer,
one step closer,
one step closer to the heart.

More frustrated every day, as the windows fall away,
and we're no closer to the day we can join our hand.
We don't have to be alone,
we can chase a dream of our own,
get away to a little home with a piece of land.
Perspectives and attitudes obscure and confuse
the plans as they're breaking apart,

oh, still we're moving one step closer,
one step closer,
one step closer to the heart.

Red lights, green lights, go back and start again,
seems like this is a game we can never win.
Puzzled by the mood, we hesitate in doubt,
while we could have so much if we'd work things out.
We keep coming and going with designs and ideas
that at the time seem smart,
Oh, but we're moving one step closer,
one step closer,
yeah, we're moving one step closer to the heart.

19

You're The One

Hard to know what you're thinking, when you get so depressed;
you just close up inside and shut out the rest.
And I wish I could just interrupt as you carry things too far,
and help you understand how important you are.

You're the one and only for my life.
Through the years, my friend and love; for all time.
In this lone, dreary world You're my bright shining sun.
You're the reason I am, Darling, you're the one.

I can't hardly say enough of my humble respect.
You just can't believe all the people you affect.
Those good times you hope for are still long overdue,
but though things seem bad now, I'm always with you.

You're the one and only for my life.
Through the years, my friend and love for all time.
In this lone, dreary world You're my bright shining sun.
You're the reason I am, Darling, you're the one.
Darling, you're the one.

20

The Best That I Can

Shall I falter and debate, only giving second rate,
never much more than what's asked for in the plan?
Never stand for a belief, run away to quick relief,
never doing the best that I can.

If I've only one time to make it here in life,
I need to stop and face things in my stand.
Though it won't measure with their side, in my heart I'll know I've
tried,
and I was doing the best that I can.

Help me give without question and freely to the need.
Let me see all my problems to get through.
Let me one at a time, break them down to my line
to see a reason and a purpose for all that I do.

If I fall on my face while running in my race,
undiscouraged, I'll start over where I began.
Although I never place a name, I'll still make it there the same,
and arrive doing the best that I can.

Let me willingly do all that's wanted of me.
Help me know that my home is with you.
Lift me high over my pride that I might look down inside
to see a reason and a purpose for all that I do.

Shall I falter and debate, only giving second rate,
fall behind, and then just hide between the span?
No, I think not anymore, there's too much left in store
to gain by doing the best that I can.

2I

I Got Hooked

I shouldn't have asked her for that dance.
I was just passing through by chance.
She seemed so lonely, by herself, waiting for Mister someone else.
I shouldn't have danced like we'd met before,
because she seemed to like how we moved over the floor.
Her perfumed hair addled up my mind,
and I lost my balance as her eyes met mine.

I was thinking, "Never Again,"
but I got hooked, and she reeled me in.
She must have known what I was thinking of,
I got hooked, and I fell in love.

I shouldn't have held her hand in mine.
Her touch stirred deep feelings inside.
Exchanging smiles and there we were, her with me and me with
her.
I shouldn't have touched her hand at all,
I'm sure that's when I started to fall.
Soon I was saying things and doing funny stuff,

and I couldn't seem to get enough.

I was thinking, "Never Again,"
but I got hooked, and she reeled me in.
She must have known what I was thinking of,
I got hooked, and I fell in love.

I shouldn't have kissed her on her front lawn,
but I thought, "There's nothing serious going on."
She seemed so sad like this was really the end,
but smiled as I asked to see her again.
And I shouldn't have kissed her, or let her turn my head,
I should have just went home and gone to bed.
But instead, I just happened in by chance
and I fell in love with that girl at the dance.

I was thinking, "Never Again,"
but I got hooked, and she reeled me in.
She must have known what I was thinking of,
I got hooked, and I fell in love.

2 2

Us (They're Only People)

You'll never find a soul open at twelve,
neither one nor two is near.
They're either out to lunch or in their cars,
or in a tavern having a beer.
But they haven't the time to stop in their tracks
to notice the people about.
Pretend you don't see them, you fear they might find out
what you're hiding that don't know about.

They're only people, people,
only people.
And they're lonely people.
Dying
in the world in which they live.
And they're crying
for the love that you can give.

You can hide from your neighbors,
forget about your friends.
Hibernate in your houses

till you come to your deadly end.
But to know yourself completely, you must truly know man.
With the love you apply you will learn,
all are searching like you to find out what it is,
that balance that keeps us in turn.

They're only people, people,
only people.
And they're lonely people.
Dying in the world in which they live.
And they're crying
for the love that you can give.
Crying
in the world in which they live.
And they're dying
for the love that you can give.

23

My Morning Memory

In my life and times gone by,
there's been so much that I've gone through.
Yet those sterling, treasured moments that shine
are my choice times spent with you.
Though most my days are spent away from your side,
in places I'd rather not be,
still part of you is carried with me inside
to reflect on at times of need.

And I live my life in love,
through the years and wherever I'll be.
I'm so much a part of all you are,
and you're so much a part of me.
Hand in hand we face tomorrow with hopes,
and when I can't be next to thee,
I still carry you deep in my heart
as my morning memory.

From my wakening hour you're with me held fast,
until the time I need to leave.

All I've learned, from what we've shared in the past
is a part of all I am and all I'll be.
When we arrive in the autumn of our days,
sharing time as best we could,
we can remember all the love in our hearts
looking back, we'll know that it was good.

And I live my life in love,
through the years and wherever I'll be.
I'm so much a part of all you are,
and you're so much a part of me.
Hand in hand we face tomorrow with hope,
and when I can't be next to thee,
I still carry you deep in my heart
as my morning memory.

24

Little Victories

We try so hard to let them know
that we still love them and support them as they grow.
Yet we pass up golden opportunities
because we're tired or we don't quite feel at ease.
Sharing time and trying just by getting all involved,
reaches out to the love and gets that problem solved.

It's those little victories in our home
that draws us closer to each other and our own.
It's the little victories we sacrifice,
that we will value and remember all our lives.

We want so much to let them know the how and why,
but wait till too much time and love has passed us by.
We want to change the world but don't know where we are.
We still won't see that it all starts in our back yard.
We span the globe to work but our children are alone.
What good are heroes if they never do come home?

It's those little victories that shed the light,

and reaffirm that all we do is good and right.
It's all the little victories we sacrifice,
that we will value and remember all our lives.

We keep waiting for the big chance to come,
so, we're caught up in the race that can't be won.
The love is worth the sacrifice we compromise
yet we don't see all the truth before our eyes.
The little touch; that common interest that we share,
the moment saved and given; shows how much we care.

It's those little victories in life,
that say it's good to share out talents and our time.
It's the little victories we sacrifice,
that we will value and remember all our lives.

25

All God's Children

The hurt you're feeling now will pass with time.
A lesson learned must have its price.
While everything seems so much out of place,
it's hard to see things ever turning right.
Though everyone has left you standing alone,
confused and lost amongst your ways.
Your courage now to face the morning ahead
will carry you far throughout the day.

It's all right, though you're on your own.
It's all right, though you're walking down this road,
even though now you feel so alone,
all God's children must journey to get back home.

A taste of anguish lingers still in your heart.
No one relates how hard you've tried.
The disappointments and failures now seem
to overwhelm that spark inside.
You're saying things will never, ever be the same,
without some trust or peace of mind.

Determination now must push you on through
the problems that you need to leave behind.

It's all right, though you're living on your own.
And it's all right, though you're walking down this road,
and even though now you feel so alone,
all God's children must journey to get back home.

Journey high, journey low,
try to seek wisdom wherever you go.
Journey far, journey wide;
try to keep the best you've learned inside.

And though foreboding signs may appear in your sky,
just reach for help and let the bad pass by; you'll be fine.

The hurt you're feeling now will pass with time.
This lesson learned is nothing new,
Your time to shine is coming round real soon,
so hold on to my hand, I walk with you.

And it's all right, though you're living on your own.
And it's all right, though you're walking down this road,
even though now you feel so alone,
all God's children must journey to get back home.

26

MEMOIRS & NOTES - 22 - 'ONE STEP CLOSER TO THE HEART

One Step Closer To The Heart

(1993) – At the time I was dating Diane, I was more than a bit apprehensive of her parents; Jack and Mickey Weeks, and rightfully so. Diane's mother was detached and somewhat reserved, never looking up at me when she talked, while Diane's father was indifferent, aloof and rather unfriendly. Frankly, I did not blame them. They were protective of Diane, and I'm sure that they were suspicious of my motives, all the while silently but urgently hoping that their daughter would get over this infatuation with that reprehensible scoundrel that had seemingly crawled out from under a rock, and I'm sure their greatest hope was that I would quickly move on to better pastures.

Diane did not, and the rest is, how would you say, "history." At the time, my dad and his wife Inez were captivated with my girlfriend Diane, but her roommates, Elizabeth and Sally, were openly suspicious of me and my intentions. They felt, especially Sally, that I was in Diane's life for a brief romantic encounter before I left her suddenly and brokenhearted. Meanwhile my brothers, Ray and Richard were taking bets on how soon it would be before Diane and our relationship would be ending. They only saw the outer shell of a young girl; not strikingly attractive like the women they gravitated towards, they therefore could not see what I saw in her. They could not see the lovely wonderfulness and the distinguished, almost hidden beauty in her that I did. They did not experience the innocence and sweetness that I craved to be next to every time we were apart.

In a way I was glad that her brilliant magnificence was hidden from other guys' views; she had captured my heart and I was not wanting to have to compete for her with anyone else, although I knew the treasure I had found and I would fight to the death to keep her in my life and in my heart. Still, in spite of the attitudes of everyone around us that continued to confuse and disorient us, we plodded on together, and although our relationship suffered to some degree as we divided at times, we followed our dreams and each other, and we kept moving closer to the heart.

Side Note:

I felt, and probably rightfully so, a bit at fault for breaking up the girl's club in the first apartment that Diane shared with Sally and Elizabeth. It was only my hope to be able to see her, that's all, but I was being denied access by Sally and I had to keep trying to be involved.

Another Side Note:

As the syncopation seemed to pull me into the essence of the song and as the harmonica played at the end of this piece was firing on most of its 20 cylinders, I felt that I had surpassed my expectations for the end results of this piece; and I was happy.

You're The One

(1991) – Sometimes, just like all of us, Dee would suddenly get depressed and despondent, not valuing the wonderfulness of herself as a person or even at times, she would question the gentle strength she brings into our relationship. It was one of those moments that I sat with her as she cried, over what seemed like, something trivial, and I consoled her with honest reassurances of her value to me, and the rest of the world, I eventually talked her out of her blue funk. That night I thought, it'd be nice if I could capture the essence of that whole thing in a song. I remained there for a few minutes and then got up, wrote some of the things I had said to her that day, and then tried to combine the mess with rhyming words. This is the result.

Side Note:

It is not unusual for the poetry to have more than one direction as it steps out into the universe. In a way, I felt it was my own song or collection of songs or maybe it was the essence of my creativity talking to me, saying that I've got to stop letting my injured ego thing affect how I approach my gifts and talents, and stop worrying whether or not Lord Baldwin will ever be recognized in the cosmos, stop comparing other's greatness's to myself; they are who and what they are, with or without me in the mix. It is good that I share my cassettes with all those people out there; it's the right thing to do when I can put my very own candle on a candlestick; and it giveth light unto all that are in care to take part in the Lord Baldwin Happening. And I need to shed light on more of my own ideas, notions, philosophies, and designs and create what only I can create with the certain and specialized gifts and talents that only I was given by my Heavenly Father. I am the one that journey's down this path, I am the reason all of these songs and all of these albums exists; I am the one.

The Best That I Can

(1977) – In the 70s there was an Latter Day Saint musical play with words and music by Doug Stewart and Lex de Azevedo called "*Satur-day's Warriors*" that was really popular. I set out to write a musical of my own, and this was one of the songs. In that scene, there is a young man that is confused because of his mother's anger with the church and he is struggling with his direction in life, questioning his own abilities and doubting his own testimony. After he prays, he realizes his calling and sings this song.

There were other songs and a good plot to go with them, but I lacked the supporting motivational drive to put it all together. With little interest or moral support by my family and friends, and with me doubting my own capabilities, lacking that certain fire that I needed to push forward to do this project, the whole thing never came together and the play never materialized. But the other songs to be included did eventually end up on different albums to follow.

Side Note:

Sometimes I'm frustrated with the knowledge that there are people doing so much with their talents and capacities, while I plod along doing whatever. But the sheer volume of my works contradicts that slippery-slope logic and faulty knowledge altogether and when one or two songs shine so much brighter than others, doesn't diminish the value of the lesser than songs nor does it diminish my own meager accomplishments, and I think at times that because I do the best I can with what I have, it is enough. And it's okay to stive for something seemingly impossibly unachievable; it helps to reach for the stars and ultimately, it builds character.

I Got Hooked

(1993) – If you'll excuse the pun, this song, using "fishing" references has a good hook; "I was thinking, 'Never Again,' but I got hooked, and she reeled me in. She must have known what I was thinking of, I got hooked, and I fell in love." Therein lies the possibly uncertain path followed by most of us to an unexpected but anticipated love. There is this course, a seemingly uncertain direction that we all seem to, step by step, follow down, in hopes that by chance, something more and wonderful will happen. This song is about one of those times that it does. Innocently enough, first he says that he shouldn't have asked her to dance and then he shouldn't have touched her and finally, he shouldn't have kissed her. Isn't that just the way it is?

Us (They're Only People)

(1974) – Diane and I had just been evicted from our apartment on the NW side of Portland; the Estelle Court Apartments where we had lived from the day we got married. We moved into the Chinese Castle off of SE 17th and Hawthorne. It's late November and we have no utilities in our new apartment. To make matters worse, Diane goes into labor and we take a taxi to the Emanuel Hospital. They tell me that we have all day and that I should just go home and come back in the early evening. So, I headed home and tried to get things set up for that time when Diane would come home with the new baby. I was at an outside phone booth a few blocks away, attempting to get ahold of the natural gas company, the telephone company, the Portland electric company, and my landlady; all to no avail.

It was lunchtime and there was a lot of people driving up and down Hawthorne Boulevard. The telephone booth that I was using was right out in front of a local tavern, and everyone seemed so busy. After a while, it seemed to me that the cars were going up and down, all with no destination, just moving somewhere because they had a need to travel.

The people walking the streets were in their own hurry, passing me by and all but ignoring me as they went on their busy way. I thought, "why are they all so afraid of each other? Aren't we all in a not so remote way, brothers and sisters?" And I thought, couldn't we all step out of the seemingly

The Chinese Castle
SE Portland Oregon

senseless crowds to see that we are all a part of this collective multitude? Perhaps maybe most of these people are just as lonely and scared as I am of them, and perhaps we could all meet together somewhere in the middle.

Later I got the phone in the Chinese Castle to work and then called the hospital to say hello to Diane. The attending nurse informed me that she was already in the operating room having the baby. I got on my bike and peddled as fast as I could over to the hospital that was miles away. After throwing my bike in the ivy on the side of the hospital, I ran up the stairs and darted around a corner to find, at that very moment, the nurses wheeling out a baby in a plastic bassinette. It was our Loren Frances, born just minutes before my arrival. I was kind of angry that I missed her birth, especially because prior to the birth I had taken the Lamaze classes to be ready for this happening, but the spirit washed over me as I looked into that bassinette at me daughter with awe and wonder.

My Morning Memory

(1985) – This is a special song written for my mother, about the bond held throughout my early days and carried throughout my adult years. I was infatuated with a song by John Denver called morning bells and kind of fashioned the tune to this song from that piece, but this song quickly took on a personification of its own. This song came from the thought that in a way, my actions, my marriage, and my children, all became a part of my mother, and that my actions and reactions were a direct result of the fact that I was a part of my mother. It was my hope to grasp the essence of being the child led by the adult only to later on reverse the roles. In a small way I hoped this song could say, "I love you and appreciate all you did for me" to my mother. Funny thing is, I don't know anybody that caught on what this song was really all about unless I would tell them, and then they would say, "oh yeah. I get it now."
Side Note:
after writing this song, which was written just before I left the

funeral home in 1985, I sent a copy of it to my mother in hopes that she might understand that I in fact, not only understood what she went through to get me through my turbulent childhood, but that I appreciated all that she did. But, if she comprehended what this song meant, it was never acknowledged, and I just moved on to the next song.

Another Side Note: At the end of summer in 1996, all of my mother's children were called to her side after she had taken a turn for the worse from her cancer and had become deathly ill. I knew that before she left this earth, I needed to tell her what I meant to tell her in this song, but the opportunity kept falling away from one incident to another. One evening, in the hospital, after the nurse let us know that she, my mother, would probably be going to sleep, we all prepared to leave. Everyone was exhausted from the hospital scenario of coming and going up and down the elevators, in and out of her room and the cafeterias and walking the hallways, waiting and playing cards, speculating on the nature of things and her prognosis. As they were all packing up and heading back to mother's home to get some rest and rejuvenate for the next day's onslaught, as exhausted as I was, I thought that this may be that moment that I needed, and I waved everyone off and went back up to her room.

Mother was a bit groggy from the drugs as she looked up and smiled at me from her hospital bed, and I told her that I brought my guitar to play her a song. I also told her that I would probably play until she fell asleep. She gave and excepting smile and I started playing songs; a lot of songs from the list that I had brought with me. When I got to this song, "My Morning Memory,"

and started playing it, tears came in my mother's eyes, and it was at that moment that I realized that even though she never wrote me back to tell me that she understood this song that I had written for her, or even listened to it, it was at that moment that I realized she knew—she knew all along. And the thought of her understanding, brought tears to my eyes and made me start choking on the words to this song as I played my guitar. I found myself playing a lot of guitar music while I was trying to compose myself.

After I finished the song I sat down with my guitar and went over to her side and whispering in her ear, poured out my heart, telling her how sorry I was to have caused all the grief to her when I was younger. With the restrictive tubes in her mouth going down her throat, she was unable to verbally say anything, but I will never forget what she conveyed with her eyes as she looked back at me, smiling approvingly.

Two days later she was gone and although I felt like I had so much more to say and so much more I wanted to hear from her, I was truly grateful for that special moment that we both had to share.

Little Victories

(1991) – Finding joy and fulfillment in the little moments that shape not only my life, but the lives of others have illusively been my goal. I have devoted a lot of time to the raising up of my children, but it's never been easy, and because Diane and I chose to have a large family, there have been a lot of sacrifices. Moreover, I think of all the wonderful things that I would like to do with them collectively and singularly, but I never seem to have the resources to follow through with any of it. This song I suppose, is more of a wish than anything else that I can appreciate the little things I do as a parent will make a difference in my home and that the real essence of family life is the love that is shared between each other, the acceptance of others faults, and a commonality or purpose for our family goals. The other thing that occurred to me was that through example they might go for, and perpetuate, a goodness to be shared with each other as family as well as with others outside in the real world to help make a loving difference in their lives.

Diane's good heart and willingness to sacrifice everything for her family is the testimony to that hope that I have to be like her. And then when I see my own children doing little good deeds for their brothers and sisters, seeing the love abound and moreover, returned back to the giver; that is a strong affirmation to me and my heart that we are doing something, not only right, but spiritually eternal. And that deed need not always be that huge occurrence or happening that cannot help but make a difference, to move and shape the destiny of all these people in my home; ofttimes it's that little, small, almost insignificant deed that might happen one time, or maybe on a daily basis and that deed testifies of the love one has for another, that we care and love each other, and not for that one moment, but for always.

Side Note:

One day I was walking through the campus at The Evergreen State College on my way to class when I saw a poster out in front of the library and I came home that night and surprised my daughters, Elizabeth and Meridith with tickets to go with me to see a ballet downtown at the Washington Center for The Performing Arts. The ballet was to be done to the Scheherazade Symphonic suite by Nikolai Rimsky-Korsakov. I was hard pressed to find the money for three tickets even though I was still a student along with my daughters, but I really felt like it was something I needed to do to bond more closely with these two teenage daughters. Also, buying the tickets early on, I secured center seats in the third row. Personally, I was excited to hear a real live orchestra playing one of my favorite pieces by Rimsky-Korsakov; Scheherazade. We got there early and the girls, sitting on either side of me, couldn't have been more excited; the sights and sounds of the other people arriving to take their seats, the great hall and stage center itself that had just finished being remodeled a few years earlier from a movie theater, originally built as the Liberty Theater in 1924 and restored to its glory; it was in a word, epic.

When the ballet got underway, I realized (and was disappointed) that there was no live orchestra, (as the prices for the tickets reflected), but instead, the ballet had canned music piped throughout the theatre.

But as I turned to whisper my disappointment to Liz, I was an amazement reflected in her face. I turned to Meridith and saw the same wonder and awe in her face too. It was then that I realized the wonderful thing I was doing. We were so close to the stage that we could hear the feet of the dancers as they moved across the stage. We were so close that we could see the sweat on the faces of the dancers as they moved through their performance.

Afterwards, we went to a local Tumwater hangout called Cattin's Restaurant and had sodas and a double order of French fries, and talked about that breathtaking ballet that we had just experienced. The laughter and excitement in their voices as we sat there was priceless. I thought about some of the other people there at that ballet that went to those performances on a regular basis and wondered if they went through what I was going through every time or did it lust become another event. As the event was reviewed and retold to Diane, I knew it didn't matter what and how things went for other folks, what mattered was my time with my girls.

All God's Children

(1984) – Sometime prior to the writing of this song, my friend Tony related a story to me about his sister Sue, who, after being consumed in a depression of hopelessness, attempted to commit suicide. Sue had a loving home, good parents that understood and loved her, she had friends and moreover she was a very attractive girl. There was a big confusion after this happened followed by counseling, therapy, not just for her but for the whole family. Tony shared with me later, some of her off track thoughts and ideas that were going through her head afterwards and before, and I'm happy to say that she pulled out of it and is now happily married with children and a loving husband. But this song was written for her and reflected some of her misgivings and concerns just prior to that happening. I wanted her to know that we cannot always know our purpose while here on earth, but we need to know that we are all important and an extraordinary part of some grander scheme. I wanted her to know that sometimes we just need to hold on and look to find out what that thing is.

Side Note:

It was my night off from working at Forest Funeral Home; Gary Rook, the managing Funeral Director, had the responsibility of being the "Call" guy should we get a call to pick up the remains of someone that passed away. (Besides the grave digger that was on call when we needed him, there was only two of us working there at Forest Funeral Home, serving as funeral directors, embalmers, family counselors, etc.) A "call" was a funeral home term to mean, the person responsible for completing the removal process and then doing the subsequent paperwork. In those days Gary and I, had these devices called, beepers, that would beep and then leave a phone number for us to call back to our answering service who would then give us all the information we needed to make the call.

With a syrupy note of superiority, she sweetly said, "Look, if you can't get over here now, I'll just call Batstone's Funeral Home and have them make the removal and you can just pick the remains up there." Batstone's was a competing funeral home in Shelton, 30 miles away, and I knew that if they made the removal, Forest Funeral Home would have to pay them $125.00 for the call.

"I'll be right there." I said dryly and hung up. After explaining the circumstances to the manager at the theater, he gave me two tickets to come back and see the movie at another time. I then boogied over to the funeral home and grabbed the 1965 Cadillac hearse that had a special gurney in the back and as we drove to St Pete's, made plans for Chet to stay in the car while I made the removal. He was cool with that until we got there and decided he wanted to go with me instead. I knew my way around the hospital and the service entrances so I was there in the morgue in less than 5 minutes. Chet stayed out in the hallway and I went inside the morgue where the caretaker or custodial person in charge of the facility showed me to the vault and slid out the drawer. Seeing the deceased was a big man, I asked if the caretaker could help me put the remains on my gurney, but was told that it wasn't in his job description. After I struggled with the heavy person, I secured his remains and covered him up with the carpet tarp and the caretaker had me sign for the removal.

The thing I was not getting was that all this time, the hearse, the gurney, the hospital, the fact that there was a dead body in the back of the vehicle we were traveling in; I was too busy trying to make this thing I was doing seem like just another job, but I was too busy to notice that Chet, sitting over from me, was silently but was terrified of the whole process. This came to a head

when we arrived at the funeral home, it was dark, and as we drove through a part of the cemetery, a rabbit ran out from one headstone to another. "I just saw something." Chet yelled.

"That's just Bugs Bunny." I said calmly. "He lives out there some-where."

"In one of the graves?" Chet replied anxiously.

I assured Chet that it was all good as I backed the vehicle into the garage. As I was getting the remains situated in the prep room, Chet, not wanting to just sit in the hearse by himself followed me in, and I thought he was okay by then, and maybe he was, until I asked him to turn on a light by the wall. As he did so, his hand seemed to brush up against or slightly touch the toe of the dead man, who was now covered with a sheet, but Chet's face turned a pale white and as he seemed to be teetering, I was afraid he was going to faint, so I walked him out to our Plymouth station wagon, drove it with him in it up to the garage and turned on the radio while I quickly went back into the prep room, secured and locked everything up. He was a lot better on our way home and I thought I was okay, but when Chet explained to Diane, in his own words what had happened, after she carefully put Chet to bed, she returned and gave me the riot act.

I have another story that I may relate later, but what you might want to know is, when Gary found out I had to make one of his calls, he told me he was sorry and that he had dropped the beeper in the toilet and it stopped working. He also let me know that the nurse I had interacted with was friends with the people at Batstone's and that he understood that they were giving her a cut in the money should they make the removal.

Oh, one other thing. Couple weeks later, I attempted to take Chet to the "Ghostbusters" movie, but he said he didn't want to see it anymore.

27

~

- 23 - SHIFTED
GEARS - 1993

28

NOTES ABOUT THE COVERS

Notes About The Covers

Note On The New Cover: For the new cover I used a panel of clock-works behind and put a gearbox to a Chrysler transmission; on top. The effect is a lot of gears and ultimately, shifted gears. I finished it off with the Bell Bottom font in likable gold or bronze colored lettering on the top and metal-colored lettering on the bottom.

Notes On The Original Covers:

I know, I know,... There was nothing wrong with the originals and I could have easily used it, but at the time my original covers were corrupt and I couldn't get them to load or even be recognized,...

So when I was putting this chapter together I scanned all of my documents (and I have a lot of redundancy),... and I finally found a good copy of the older covers and saved the working copies in more than a few places to therefore have them saved,... and I could totally use either one of them for the back cover if it was ever so needed.

29

SHIFTED GEARS

Shifted Gears
Little People
Bobcat Ridge
Now Is The Time For Our Test
Time To Move On
Doing This The Right Way

"Shifted Gears," Copyright © November, 1993,
All Rights Reserved

30

Shifted Gears

Hey, I worked the shipyards; an electrician union man.
I labored with lifers that didn't have a clue or plan.
The money was there, benefits were fair,
but I needed to get out,
to find myself and figure what I was all about.

So I shifted gears and I jumped the track,
took a long hard look from a long way back.
I stopped judging my life from the eyes of my peers,
my life got better since I shifted gears.

Hey, the family and relatives criticized what we planned to do.
but they couldn't see things from our point of view.
No, they just couldn't believe, said I was crazy to leave,
and wondered how we'd make ends meet,
predictions were made on how soon
we'd all be in the streets.

But still, I shifted gears and I jumped the track,
I took a long hard look from a long way back.

I stopped judging myself from the views of my peers,
and started living again after I shifted gears.

We both had our worries too; financially in a mess,
we both felt that there had be more to life
than all this stress.

Hey, I left the shipyard,
I'm now working at the "Get It And Go."
I'm doing what I want; going where I want to go.
Yeah, a better life each day with Jake and Rene,
looking forward to the oncoming years.
Less tension; more contentment,
after shifting down;
shifting down the gears.

Yeah, I shifted gears and I jumped the track,
I took a long hard look from a long way back.
I stopped judging myself from the views of my peers,
and started living again after I shifted gears.

31

Little People

The little people are everywhere;
no need to search to find them there.
Bouncing on beds and running the halls,
hiding in cupboards or writing on walls,

lounging on couches, watching TV,
under the house or up in a tree.
They're under my feet and in my way,
with all the world to do and say.
They're a curious lot; they cling and pursue,
copying everything I do.

The little people have sharp minds
and come in both male and female kinds.
A variety of sizes, older and new,
with an attitude that they're just passing through.

They run a pace like today won't keep,
then all of a sudden, they fall fast asleep.
The logic and reason seem to be lost,

but they manage in spite of the wires all crossed.
Smiling, well mannered, they seem sincere,
yet, I wonder how long they'll all be staying here.

The little people are wild and free,
they follow no patterns that I can see.
Mistakes are their nature most of the time,
and they act without thinking, reason or rhyme.

I've studied their methods and validity
of possible deductive reasoning.
By now my conclusions should come to no shock,
they defy all the rules and are a paradox.
I'm not surprised, though a bit perplexed,
I can never predict what they'll do next.

The little people have touched my heart,
and fulfill something of a missing part.
It's like old friends joined together again,
or a reminder of what I might have been.

They trust me to lead, that I should know best,
a pleasant kindness to receive from a guest.
They help me feel special, with purpose and cause,
and want to share all my habits and laws.
This joy can't be contained or bound,
I think I'm going to keep them around.

32

Bobcat Ridge

I couldn't wait to get away from that one-horse town.
Move out on my own
and start to really get around.
And it's funny how life is better down the road, far away,
till from miles gone by, you look back
from where you came.

Many years and miles have found me at this place.
A far cry from home. Too far, too long, too late.
And I think of that life and all the things we did,
when we were young and innocent,
up on Bobcat Ridge.

I left Suzanne waiting while I had to find myself.
I imagine after all these years
she's with somebody else.
I still regret my leaving her, and I sometimes wonder why,
but I can not change the past
and all the time that passed by.

Many years and miles have found me at this place.
A far cry from happy in this treadmill race.
But I think back at times, all the things we did,
when we were young and innocent
up on Bobcat Ridge.

Some have measured my success by my station in life,
how much money's in the bank
and the car that I drive.
But they can not see the man that sacrificed and lost it all,
who's one wish is to go back
to a place, now long gone.

Too many years and miles have found me at this place,
And I'm a far cry from happy. Too far, too long, too late.
But there's times I think back, when I was a kid,
and I'm there with all my friends
up on Bobcat Ridge.
Bobcat Ridge.

33

Getting By

"It's only money," my Dad would say, and, "money's to be spent."
Yet he'd count every nickel away, and still wonder where it all went.
He had his method, a plan of sorts and we never questioned why.
But he could have set up classes on the art of getting by.

And as time went on I'd see there was a balance to all of the needs.
All of my regrets and remorse for that uneasy course
fell away in the wisdom of why, we were getting by.

Now with family of my own, I've spent years with little gain.
Doing so much with so little, I'm too occupied to complain.
Using substitutes, fixing what's broke, making due with what'll fly,
and wondering how long we'll continue this life of getting by.

And as time goes on, I see, there's a balance to all of the needs.
All regrets and remorse for our uneasy course
fall away in the wisdom of why, we're here getting by.

We know the state of affairs can be a full or an empty purse,
but we can't know if in our future we'd be better off or worse.

As life goes on, we tend to look back and maybe wonder why
we did what we did from day to day and only managed to get by.

And as time goes on, I see, there's a balance to all of the needs.
All regrets and remorse for our uneasy course
fall away in the wisdom of why, we has to be getting by.

We could justify conditions, rationalize for each defeat,
or maybe marvel just a little bit, on how we've made ends meet.
Necessity teaches resourcefulness as we learn adversity's fight,
being stronger and with wisdom act with the skills of getting by.

And as time goes on, I see, there's a balance to all of the needs.
All of our regrets and remorse for this uneasy course
fall away in the wisdom of why, we're here, getting by.

34

Now Is The Time For Our Test

The service I'm devoted to has called to me and I must go;
I know for you this is hard.
But all my life I've waited for a chance to prove my total worth
and I know that now this is right.
I must journey now in the dark cool dawn,
keep in mind while I am gone,
I'll carry our love with my quest.
Don't forget to write; don't forget to pray,
keep in mind while I'm away;
now is the time for our test.

I must go to do my Father's work.
It's been preordained for me and I won't fail.
Though I must fight for what we both know is right,
I may not see you till I call your name through the veil.

In your eyes I see you understand,
but yet you turn away your hand;

still, like me, you know this is best.
And all those promises and covenants
we made long ago to last through time;
well, now is the time for our test.

Again, I go to do my Father's work.
It's been preordained for me and I won't fail.
Though I might die and never see your face in this life,
I may not see you till I call your name through the veil.

Come and give to me your best kiss;
try not to show how much you'll miss me,
then go back to sleep and get some rest.
And all that love we vowed should never die
will stand strong like the Rock of time,
for now is the time for our test,
I feel that now is the time for our test.

35

Time To Move On

We can learn from mistakes; try to be fair,
pick up the pieces and go from there.
We can accept the truth; try to go with the flow,
knowing what's done is done and let it all go.

But we can't make up for lost time,
It's already gone, it's already gone.
Only, learn from the past
and know it's time to move on.

As we harbor illusions; could be heartaches in store.
If we embrace lies we'll only fool ourselves more.
Yesterday's dead, still your dream is alive.
Now is the moment to get on with your life.

But we can't make up for lost time;
it's already gone, it's already gone.
Still, we learn from the past
and know it's time to move on.

Forward and onward; pushing ahead,
trying to make sense of it before I'm dead.

Everything is behind us; the future's in place.
Looking at tomorrow as the challenge to face.
People out there in need, confused by the fall,
need our help in sharing what we can do for them all.

But we can't get back all the lost time,
It's already gone, it's already gone.
Yet we can learn from the past
and know it's time to move on.
Yet we can learn from the past
and know it's time to move on.

36

Doing This The Right Way

Still can't understand what's happening to us all,
after all these years of pushing against the wall.
Fighting the system and stepping over the line,
got me nowhere, and in trouble most the time.

So now, here I am, in your mainstream flow,
and somehow negotiating within areas, I don't know.
And now this love is taking over my heart,
I'm somewhat in change, but I've liked it from the start.

It's seems to me to be so strange
I never thought that I'd be the one to change.
I'm having so much fun, it's like I'm at play,
and yet here I am; doing this the right way,
doing this the right way.

Still can't understand what's happening to you and me,
after all this time and the way things used to be.
But now, here you are, with my love, in my life,
sharing the bathroom, with these kids, as my wife.

So now, here I am, with plans that will come to be,
and wondering why it took me so long to finally see.
And now, this love is taking over my heart,
and I would never want to tear this thing apart.

It's seems to me to be so strange
I never thought that I'd be the one to change.
Everything is coming together, day by day,
and still, here I am, doing this the right way.
Doing this the right way.
Doing this the right way.

37

MEMOIRS & NOTES - 23 - 'SHIFTED GEARS'

Shifted Gears

(1993) – In the late '70s, I worked with this eclectic, off the wall kind of guy named Bob Smulkowski nicknamed Ski, who was a veteran of the Vietnam War and was in transition while he was working at for a time at JW Electronics. Right about the time we became good friends, the Veterans Administration along with another government agency arranged for him to become an electrician up in the shipyards in Bremerton.

I lost track of him until maybe three years later when we bumped into each other in a parking lot of grocery store. He told me about the escapades of working in Bremerton shipyards and the general apathy of all the other people they worked with.

Well, I kept in contact with them a little bit here and little but there a lot of time went by and one day I met him, his wife and their baby boy in grocery store. He told me that he finally just quit

the whole shipyards thing. He said that it didn't really matter that he had great benefits and good pay, he was just not happy there. And so, he and his wife started working at a little convenience store out by Steamboat Island called, "Get It And Go." Once again Ski was happy and felt that life was good again. It was from his joy that I chose to write this song and afterwards I gave him a copy of this song, and the rest of the album and told them that he had moved me enough to write this song.

Side Note:

Years later Ski started working about four blocks away from the college at an alternator rebuilding facility and I went over and visited him a couple times while trying to revive my 1967 Chevy Nova. As a kind of ego thing, I asked about the album and without embarrassment, he told me, "I lost that tape a long time ago and I don't remember much about it." That kind of took the wind out of my sails, but I love him anyways. Recognizing that life and the pursuit of happiness is much more and there are other meanings to existence than the job and the work you do to support yourself.

Another Side Note:

I been riding bicycles my whole life and got my first ten-speed in 1971 at Meyer & Franks and got my dad's discount. That bike got stolen at Portland State University. I was hooked on the shifted gears and bought another right after I went back to work.

Yet Another Side Note:

When I was putting music to this composition I wanted to try something different. I decided to use the keys of the notes for the natural tuning of a guitar. That would be, E, A, D, G, B, and E, so the chords began with E major, then over again to E major then A major, then D major, then G major, then B major then back to E major. Into the chorus with; B major to E major, again B major to E major, C# minor to A major, then to F# minor, back to E major. Kind of weird, but it did work and with a funky percussion in the background it worked.

And Yet Again, Another Side Note:

Just recently I was in contact with Bob who told me that he has worked for the State for almost 21 years... and was getting ready to retire this coming spring, and I guess he and Renee will be heading out to northern Idaho where his son Jake (sonny boy) and his girl and their grandson are presently living. I do wish him well.

Little People

(1989) – For better or worse, this is a subject I have a lot of experience in. The premise of this song was almost as if you had a hermit that had never experienced children and in fact could not remember his own childhood, suddenly thrown in with his family that had many of these little people all around. Being on familiar terms with and observing closely, those amazing or astonishing beings (our children), that reside, grow and develop in their habitats, (our homes). Imagine all the subtleties to this experimental laboratory. These interactions and his observations are the key to the success and the feel of what I was trying to say in this song. Of course, the logical choice after an interaction and observation and analyzing of his surroundings would be that of a positive nature, but I reminded all the time, at work, at school, and even at church that there are some people that do not like and choose not to interact with children for the exact same reason that the hermit chooses to.

Side Note:

Okay, not gonna lie; life at the baldwin house was crazy while financially; not that good. Things at JW Electronics had gotten worse with no chance of pulling out of the tailspin we were in. By this time, most of the reps were gone, most of the outside salesmen were gone, all but two of the counter  sales persons were gone, as well as most of the other employees in the back room. The general disposition of my father-in-law was disheartening but understandable for a guy that had built up a business from nothing and accomplished creating such a multi-state multimillion-dollar electronic sales empire that lasted for 25 years. And we were in some holding pattern; with the business in hard times, I can't be going anywhere; I can't jump ship (like everyone else) and leave my father-in-law to struggle with his business like that. One word; Family.

And speaking of family; while this was all happening at work, Christopher was now seven months old who, two years later would attach himself to his brother Chet, 13, and follow him around wanting to be a part of Chet's gang of friends.

Ben, seven, and Stephen, five, were thick as thieves; the best of buddies and friends doing everything together, and joined ofttimes by Spencer, almost three, who just knew whatever they were doing would be alright with him. And those three musketeers were always pushing the limits and getting in trouble, (and blaming Spencer for the damage when they could). I might mention, there were two sets of bunkbeds in the garage, (we called the garage, the boy's room), where Chet, Ben, Stephen, Spencer and Christopher, (on a pull-out trundle bed), all slept, hung out, watched movies together, (on a small 13-inch monitor), and played the Atari computer in their lair.

Meridith, nine, had decided that she would be pursuing a life in the theatre, (we always knew she would), and with a beautiful clear voice, would be singing songs with or without requests, she would also embellish her performances with her dancing and loved to extent the finalities to all of her performances.

Liz, eleven, was now into a lot of the same music that her sister Lori, 15, was listening to and she could sometimes be found in Lori's room with Lori, listening to music while she or both of them did homework or their hair.

On December second, I took Lori and Chet to the Tumwater Football State Championship game that was held in the Kingdome in Seattle. Lori insisted on sitting somewhere else with her friends and I did have my eye on where she was, but at the end of the game; the crowd erupted, and students were everywhere and Lori was not where I last saw her. We had made an agreement to meet at a place but Chet and waited and she never showed. I panicked and had to leave Chet at the rendezvous point to find a phone to make a long-distance call to Diane to tell her I had lost her daughter in the Kingdome. From the phonebooth I could see scads of people pouring out of the place but did not see Lori. When Diane answered the phone, she interrupted me as I was trying to tell her what had happened and told me that Lori had called; she was crying because she couldn't fine me and Chet. And Lori was going to call back in two minutes. I reiterated our rendezvous point and went back to Chet. When Lori finally found us, I was livid and wanted to tear into her with anger, (which I've been guilty of before and sorry to say times after this) but seeing the sad, sorry look on her face I held back and Lori explained that there was another rendezvous point just like this one on the other side of the stadium. On our way home, we collectively raved about the game; Tumwater won against Cheney High School, 27 to 7, and decided it was better than the last time in 1987, when they beat, West Valley High School, anyway, all was well.

Another Side Note:

In the spring of 1948 my mother returned to Portland Oregon with two boys, John, 4, and David 3, after a failed marriage. Around that same time, my father's first marriage also ended in divorce, leaving him with two boys; Jack, 5 and Edward, 4.

My mother went to work driving a small food truck and because Grandma Scarbrough, whose house she and her boys were living in, was also working, mother found a lady named Mabel that was doing daycare close to where Grandma lived.

As life went on, my dad had his two boys dropped off during the day at his mother's until it became too much of a burden on Grandma (Azlin) Baldwin so my dad found a babysitter for his boys while he was working, driving a delivery truck for Meier & Franks, a department store in downtown Portland. That babysitter was also, Mabel.

It didn't take long for Mabel to see some very stark similarities between Mrs. Eva Keiser and Mr. Jack Baldwin. Both had just come away from messy divorces, both were close in age, my dad, 25 and my mother 24, both had two boys that were very close in age, and as Mabel had varied opportunities to talk with each person as they dropped off or picked up their children, she could feel the loneliness they were both experiencing and she knew from speaking to them on different occasions, that

The Matchmaker - Mabel

each was hoping for someone to love and each was looking for that special someone to be a good parent for their boys. One thing more, Mabel got prompted by the spirit to introduce these two to each other.

One Friday afternoon, as my dad was picking up Jack and Ed, my dad was writing a check to pay Mable for the babysitting, Mabel tells him of this beautiful woman that was about his age that was dropping off her kids every day and that she too has two boys, about the same age and, that his kids and her kids had already become good friends. She tells him if he could wait just ten minutes, he could meet her.

My Mother And My Father - 1948

My dad declined, and told her it he was still hurting from his previous marriage with Delores and that he was trying to keep his, and his kid's lives, together.

Knowing she had been spiritually inspired, Mabel then waited for my mother to pick up her boys and Mabel tells her of this handsome man that was about her age, dropping off his kids every day and that he too has two boys, about the same age and, that her kids and his kids had already become good friends. Mabel told Eva that if she would like to meet him, she would need to be there a bit earlier to pick up her kids.

That did not happen for the next few days, but the following Friday, my mother showed up early to meet this mysterious man, only to find that my dad did not show up at his designated time. Instead, he decided to come later so that he could indeed meet up with this mysterious woman.

When the two met, I'm told that sparks flew and while Mabel continued to babysit, they went bowling that same night to get to know each other.

Their courtship was not lengthy; the four boys were all for getting the gang together and my mother and father really had some chemistry between each other. They married, set up house in Portland and. spaced out a year apart from each other, they then had three more boys.

Bobcat Ridge

(1991) –I think we all leave behind us, a trail of people, places, things and memories, stuff of the past that shaped the individuals that we became or are still becoming.

Like me, I'm sure that there are many out there that wonder what ever happened to.... Or, I wonder what would have happened if...

The scenario in this song is close to my heart, although part of the fabrication has never materialized, you know, I mean like the money stuff, but I was hoping to capture the innocence of love and later the loss of innocence with the knowledge that we all grow up and away from our own personal Bobcat Ridge. Unless we're extremely happy with everything and everyone around us, and all of our needs are being met, I think we can't help but wonder what if things would have stayed the way they were, and what if we would not have moved, and what if that girl across the street or down the block that you were so infatuated with at the time, when she didn't lose contact with you? I find that there have been times where I've looked out the windows of my car and wondered what am I doing here?

Side Note:

I have a very limited audience most of the time and I find myself evaluating my creations to determine whether they're good or not so good. Yes, I have the Diane barometer, but that barometer is duly biased at times and the critic would be like I never needed to ask her. But wait, lurking in the halls and the bedrooms and the living room, or the kitchen, there are my greatest critics. Greatest because they're not afraid to say "I don't like it that way," or, or they'll lie but let you know they're lying in the way that they're speaking so I know I have to reverse whatever they say. Yes, I'm talking about my kids; and all of them would respond when I asked them. Some of the best of them were Elizabeth and Meridith.

Don't get me wrong, Chet was good too, but he wasn't around all the time like Elizabeth and Meridith were,... they were inseparably joined at the hip and always bouncing things off of each other,... and my favorite interactions with them was when I'd have them both listen to a song at the same time. Then Meridith would comment on how she liked something and Liz would agree, or maybe disagree, but then go on a different path about something else within the song, and then, like she didn't want us to think that she wasn't aware of that other thing Liz mentioned, Meridith would instantly come up with something entirely different, and sometimes it would go on and on like that. The thing is, the comments and critics were not always favorable and their thoughts and feelings became a part of that song, thoughts and feelings that remain with me today and will be in my mind forever. So you see, the things they said were important. There have been more than a few songs that went back to the drawing board to get those songs straightened out. This was one of them. When I played the song to them, I could see them both looking stoically into space and I was so happy knowing they were listening so intently. When the song ended the two girls stopped and stared into each other's faces, looking to find who would say the first thing. After a long silence, maybe 20 seconds, I said, "Okay, that means it's either too bad and nobody wants to tell me,... or, it was so good that you're having a hard time finding the right words."

They both laughed but neither ventured to say anything. A couple days later I'm visited by Liz in the music area of my bedroom where I was working on a different song. As she saunters in the room, Liz says, "You knew we both liked the song, right?" I smiled and said, "Well I wasn't sure till just now." She went on to tell me that she thought that it was one of my best songs. And to this day when I perform this piece, I'm reminded that this is one of my daughter Liz's favorites.

Getting By

(1993) – Being my father's son, I have come a long way and learned a good deal about how to get by with whatever we have. This song is taken from the context of my father and me being my father's son.

I think we all live on dreams and hopes of a better tomorrow with enough food to go around, and more then enough money for the bills so we can spend it on other things, like ice cream, and time to do things together like taking vacations and outings, and spending good, quality time with each other, but unfortunately for many, this is just a dream and an unrealized hope. I do like to think that I have become an expert at scrimping and saving, and making do with whatever we have, for as long as we need, until we have to have it replaced, and in general, I follow the admonitions of my own father, who is a master at getting by. I think I've told this story before; there was a certain time where we paid our tithing and paid our bills and afterwards had only 19 dollars to last us through to the end of the month. I went to the Mega Foods store and bought a 100-pound bag of potatoes from some guy out in the parking lot. I think I also got some pancake mix from the store also. And for the next two or three weeks, aside from pancakes every morning for breakfast, we had potatoes—fried, baked, boiled, mashed, and ant other number of combinations. The kids never complained and we celebrated afterwards with a dinner of pizza, pop and ice-cream.

Me & My Dad

Unlike my father, I have learned over time that there is a time to open up my wallet and spend a little bit of money. Certainly, more now than in the past, I have realized that this time that we spend as parents, as family members—this time only comes around once and we either do a good job or we do not. Yes there are mediocre times too, but kids grow up fast and we should do whatever we can to love them and help them to become good people.

I can't help but think that many of my children might have had to go without a little bit more than they should have and mostly because of my frugal attitude. All in all, a lot of people would like to help me justify my shortcomings, and I can feel sorry for myself well enough, but I think now that the real art of getting by is done by maintaining a balance of wants and needs, doing the best you can within that realm, honing or prioritizing your wants, differentiating them from needs, being thankful for the blessings you have, and having a hopeful attitude for the future.

Side Note:

I was working for the college, I had money coming in, but I was what was known as an eleven-month employee where I didn't work or get paid for working the last half of August till the second half of September. That meant there was no check coming in till the second half of October. We had to get creative during the opening of school for supplies and clothes, not to mention, Chet and Liz and Allison and Stephen all had birthdays that would be affected by this money drought. Meanwhile, Lori's at Western State University, so that meant Chet now had his own bedroom (Lori's) to himself, making Ben, (who is twelve), the king of the boy's bedroom.

But I want to talk about Spencer who was seven at the time. A year had gone by since Christopher's passing, and although we all went through our ways to deal with the family tragedy, I think Spencer took Christopher's passing the worst; it was really hard for him. Christopher was his little brother that, when he wasn't trying to be a part of what was going on in Chet's life, Christopher always gravitated to join and play with his big brother Spencer, who we found out later, had attention deficit disorder (ADD), but Spencer was always moving from one project to another, which appealed to Christopher as he would be seen following behind Spencer, waiting for him to be invited into Spencer's World. Christopher also could be found sleeping with Spencer in Spencer's bed at night instead of his own trundle bed.

When all of this came crashing down on us all, we had all dealt with the loss in our different ways, but Spencer just shut his feeling up inside and pretended he was okay. In the middle of the funeral services at the Puget and Yew building, when Spencer shouted out, "Okay, okay already." Diane and I took this to mean, he was done with all this morbidity. No, he didn't break down at times and cry, like I would find myself doing, and he didn't talk about it like Ben and Meridith did, and

I didn't find him alone on his bed staring into space like I found Liz doing once, in fact, he did none of those things and seemingly didn't want to talk about it at all. At seven, Spencer would keep up with whatever Stephen and Ben were doing and he was not at a loss for other friends like Michael Diaz, but there were times, little slots or moments where Spencer was not quite there and I think Diane and I talked about having him see a counselor or something, but things changed and we moved on. But I feel that the death of his little brother Christopher was the catalyst for Spencer's ongoing problems with depression, which he still deals with to this day.

Years later, after Brian was born, Spencer really wanted to have a relationship with him but I think Spencer tried too hard to bring Brian around to like him. Brian was a curious kind of kid, but Spencer was eight years older than Brian, and Spencer's interests at let's say, 12 or 13 was not as appealing to Brian at four or five. And Brian was fearful of Spencer doing a, "Power Bomb" wrestling move on him. But, let me assure you that Spencer did eventually capture Brian's heart and admiration because Brian was captivated by video games and Spencer was a master over much of what he played. And I think Spencer appreciated his little brother sitting on his bed watching him side-scroll his way through a Super Mario Brother's game or the Legend of Zelda, or Crash Bandicoot, (of which Brian himself became the master). This shared love has never ended for the boys and they all love to interact with each other for a good video game. Diane hates video games and I'm not real keen on them myself, (didn't have time for them to learn their strategies), but I am thankful for them helping to bring Brian love and interest into Spencer's circle; a win for both of them.

Now Is The Time For Our Test

(1979) – I wrote this song from three perspectives founded on some of the Church of Jesus Christ of Latter Day Saints beliefs; mainly that of service.

First, in a past perspective where Brigham Young was preparing to go on a mission, and although he and his family were extremely sick, and although he was advised by some of his family and friends that he should wait until he was better, he chose to go on his mission when it was his time to go to Great Britain.

Second, I was thinking about the many missionary men and women that believe what they're doing is right and go forth to do that work even at the condemnation of friends and even family, and perhaps dealing with their fiancés because of misunderstandings.

Third, I thought of the time when an official from the church might call and say that it is time to go and shore up the church; perhaps even without the support of their spouse, their family or their friends. It was the attitude of those that went out to serve the world, regardless of personal degradation, persecution, physical maladies or lack of support.

Side Note:

As perhaps mentioned previously, I was in the process of writing a musical play and I wrote many songs for this production that never came to pass, and this was another one of them. In the early 80s, the Olympia-Lacey Stake decided to put on a production which included the talents of the Saints in the area.

For two weeks I prepared for the audition I would go up in front of, so that I might do this song and perhaps the spirit might move those judges and allow me to play this song for them in their production. It was not to be, and

Hurrah For Israel
Painting by Robert Theodore Barrett

President Gilbert himself came up to me and said that it's not quite what they were looking for. I was duly devastated and it would be years before I would even consider writing another song with a spiritual theme, but I did.

Time To Move On

(1991) – Comprehending the necessitate to accept the failings and misfortunes of the past and stepping forward and onward into today. Okay, it's late 1993, over a year has passed, and I'm still lamenting the death of my son, Christopher. On one hand, I think that I wanted some type of knowledgeable counseling to let me know that it was normal and healthy for me to still be going through this grieving process, which would creep up on me at the

oddest times, and on the other hand, I needed to know that it was alright for me to let it go and move on. So it was, this song was written for me and to me by me.

Side Note:

During the summers in Iron Mountain, it actually did get very hot and my older brothers had a cure for it. There was Kool-Aid (5 ¢) where you had to add sugar and there was Wyler's lemonade (10 ¢), where you only had to add water. John would make a gallon of the lemonade and gave us all a chance to drink all we could be fore he promised to drain the rest. I was sure I could drink half of the gallon, but I could not. And after David and Richard had a chance, about a quart left over after John's turn.

Another Side Note:

Mother would buy the big, #10 can of Pineapple slices, open it and with a rubber

lid on top, she would leave it in the refrigerator on the back porch mud room. One hot summer day I watched as John crept into the mud room, flip the lid open, he then stuck his hand in the juice and fished out a slice of pineapple. He looked around before closing the lid and after he got outside, he had a satisfying smile on his face as he ate it.

I thought a cold slice of pineapple would be mighty good on that hot day too, so I waited till nobody was around, went on the back porch and fished out my own slice. It was just as good as I imagined it was to John. So good that I revisited the #10 can a few more times later. Besides, the pineapple juice was almost still close to the top so I was thinking nobody would miss my few slices.

Apparently, I wasn't the only one revisiting the pineapple because a few days later my mother was making an Pineapple Upside-Down cake and went to get some slices and found there was only four slices left. She called us all into the kitchen and found to all of our surprises that confessions came from John, David, Richie and myself. Mother laughed and said that she was guilt too but then asked how many of us washed our hands before we fished. There was no hands up and mother grimaced and said, "Uh,..., that's gross just to think of it." She informed us that this would be the last time that we would be able to do that, and for the rest of the summer I would pass that refrigerator, I would remember but I knew it was time to move on.

Doing This The Right Way

(1993) – Figuring out that although I may not be moving down that highway to success and fame and fortune as quickly as I might wish, and although a lot of the time I did get things wrong, I still found that as I went with my heart and love in front of me, I was doing something right, and in so doing, I was happy. This is a song that recognizes accomplishments in life and love while addressing the realization that in spite of the fact that a person may seem to be off course and goes about getting things done in the wrong way, somehow that person may still manage to come full circle and what they do or even how they do things, ends up being the right thing to do after all.

Side Note:
Towards the end of 1992, I begin a new chapter working at SPSCC and was officially given charge of my own computer lab in a classroom just inside the building 31 gymnasium complex. The whole story was,

the gym cost a lot of money, so there were private citizens that had donated money towards the gymnasium. Some of those people that had donated a *lot* of money stipulated that if they donated said money, they wanted the building to have classrooms included so as to have something else besides sports dominating the building, so three classrooms were included in the design. Also, it was a new thing; students needing a place to go to, to do their school assignments and print them out. And, believe it or not, most people did not have access to a personal computer in their homes.

The new room was set up like a classroom, with 24 computer desks, complete with chairs, an aisle in the center divided two sets of 12 computer desks each, with four desks going across on both sides of the aisle, with three rows down. The computers desks on the center aisle, six of them, each had an HP 500 printer, to be used by the four computers in that half row. The front of the room was set up like a classroom also with a table like desk, an overhead projector and in front of the class, a wall of dry marker writing boards.

Another Side Note:

I was told when I put the lab together, that it was to be a dedicated lab, but I soon found out that there were teachers, this was especially true to some of the instructors that were teaching Computer Sciences, vying to have their class taught in my new computer lab, and they did not care about the other student's wants or needs.

Prior to me opening the computer lab, on April 6, 1992, Microsoft had commenced Windows 3.1, which introduced several enhancements to the still MS-DOS-based platform, including improved system stability, expanded support for multimedia, TrueType fonts, and a workgroup networking capability. This was very important because that software did more to open up the PC world than any other software (including MS-DOS), and was the operating system that I installed on all the computers, (including a computer up at the front desk and two computers in my office).

One day, without my prior notification, an instructor came in and informed me that he was going to be teaching a class on how to use

Windows 3.1 at 11:00 Thursdays for the rest of the quarter. I went to my supervisor, Mrs. B., who apologized for not giving me prior notice and then told me that the Vice President to the college, Mike B., had made these arrangements, and to her understanding, it was only going to be a one-time thing. A year later they were doing classes in there on an informal basis and guess what? My son Chet, who was doing Running Start with Tumwater High School, and he was in one of those classes. A year after that the lab was networked and Andrew and Ray, who did not usually work during certain months came in and ran all the wiring and installed a hub. Not even a year after that, after commercial use restrictions were lifted in 1995 the computer lab had the internet. But hold your horses there, wasn't too many students that knew what to do with the internet; but that quickly changed and my lab was now hot with students wanting to play. I used to have to limit usage for 15 minutes before I'd have to kick people out so others could do their homework. I ended up managing that computer lab until 1997 when the new building 34 had been completed and I was transferred over to there.

And Yet Another Side Note:

There was a guy that was an athletic assistant that washed clothes for the coaches, managed the weight room and had an office space between the two locker rooms. One day one of the students on the basketball team told me that this fellow was stopping students and telling them to go somewhere else, and he was spreading rumors that no one was using the labs, I needed to go and that Mike B. was listening. I found out that this fellow was my union Shop Steward. After that, Mike B. requested that I keep a count on how many people were using the lab and at what times. I did this for five months but I knew it was a matter of time before I heard from Mrs. B., and sure enough she had me in her office and it happened.

Fun fact

the person that did all the campaigning to have me ousted, did end up in that classroom. He came in one day and was watching as I dismounted and disassembled all of my computer gear to be moved out with the furniture, and he gloated on how it was him that got me out of that space so he could have my office.

I found out later that he really wanted his own private office; my office, so that he could run a business on the side using the internet. He got caught doing transactions and was warned to stop it. He did not, and the second time he got written up and a letter was put in his file. I guess he did not understand that the internet police were monitoring his activities, because he continued his activities and was fired. I think it odd that he worked so hard to get me out so he could have my office, only to be in that office for less than two months.

38

❧

- 24 - NEW SUITS - 1993 -

39

⚮

NOTES ABOUT THE COVERS

Notes On The New Cover:

The new cover is a stark look down a naked Wall Street at dawn. Appropriate picture for part of the namesake. I was looking for a street filled with lots of people, in suits, but I liked this one and kept it.

Notes On The Original Covers:

The original cover appealed to me at the time because the guy sitting there maybe playing harmonica looked a lot like my brother David. I could not use this picture because if you look in the lower right-hand corner of the picture there is a copywrite notice. And the back cover is a famous painter of which I don't remember – I thought it was Henri de Toulouse-Lautrec but I couldn't find it amongst his works.

40

NEW SUITS

New Suits
It's Too Late
A Long Way To Go
Time To Decide
Come Hold Restless Ideas Seen Together
Over And Done
Bulldozer (Where Is The Love?)
Fairfax After Midnight
Song For The Road

41

New Suits

New suits are on the move,
with their red power ties and their wing tip shoes.

New suits, with so much to prove
when someone wins, somebody's got to lose.

New suits, up before the sun
formulating their plans for that work to be done.

New suits stepping in high gear
with all the right words you want to hear.
It may not be the truth, you may follow in doubt
but they never give up till the checkbooks' out.

New suits are on the go,
with their tasteful beemers in the freeway flow.

New suits, with so much to do
to make sure they win, somebody's got to lose.

New suits shuffling notes away
with a paper chase to the world today.

New suits, confident and sure
with one leg up on the meager and poor.
Speaking in platitudes and familiar clichés
and stashing six figures for some future days. Hey, hey.

New suits are in the fight,
with the confidence and poise as things get tight.

New suits, on T.V. in the news
hey, no matter who wins, they know they'll never lose.

New suits on congressional floors
as the real intrigue is rendered behind a door.

New suits playing the role
with their conflict of interests, out of control.
Opinions, conjecture from a driven, warped view
with my money and yours to carry things through.

New suits are in the show,
with lots of new faces that come and go.
New suits take in the cruise
and when they win, you know; somebody will lose.

42

It's Too Late

Whether it's wrong or right, we all justify
mistakes we made back then
for the way things should have been.
but soon it's all gone, as life goes on,
while we look back and know that it's too late.

To carry on our family way, I work all my life away,
thinking when I'm finally ahead,
I'll make it up to them again. But it's never enough
as new things come up
and one thing leads to another till it's too late.

From efforts failed in play an attitude goes array.
I seek out the quickest end
even though this is my friend,
and for the final word what really occurs
is a consequence of sorrow that it's too late.

43

A Long Way To Go

The morning finally breaks. So many stand in wait,
looking through the window, waiting for this day.
Rushing and yet lingering, they take their place in line,
and one by one they go forth to take their place in time.

The road is always traveled, by a constant, moving flow.
Some are ending their journey,
while others have a long way to go; a long way to go.

The day sees many tasks, in need of being done.
So much to accomplish, this work under the sun.
Working and yet learning, they find their place again,
and see the path before them that never seems to end.

The road, forever traveled, by the scholars in the know,
teaching while being taught,
learning while there's a long way to go; a long way to go.

The day is filled with wonder, for all who reach and see.
Some seem to pass time quickly, while for others, it's an eternity.

Work for some is swift and short, it hardly seems the dawn.
They leave for home before mid-day while others tarry on.

In eve, they walk the road again to finally reach their home.
and share the tales with family, of their long way to go;
their long way to go,... way to go.

44

Time To Decide

Some people got no reasons, others got no sense,
me, I was blessed with a little of both,
no excuse for walking this fence.

It's time to decide,
whether where I'm going is where I want to be.
It's time to decide,
what it is and to stand for what I believe.

Some people have no convictions,
others stand on the line.
I'm making little progress while I'm running out of time.

It's time to decide,
to set the goals and finally set my course.
It's time to decide,
to push in one direction; all my force.

Some people procrastinate, others just don't care.
Me, I see the wheels in turn, pulling away from there.

Time to decide,
to make the move and constitute the change.
It's time to decide,
to get in gear before I'm out of range.

Last time I saw Louie, he hadn't changed from before.
I told him my dilemma,
but he didn't want to hear any more.

"Not time to decide," He said,
"I'm not ready for a move, at this time."
"Not time to decide,
"I've lots of time to figure out my life."

And I said, hey Louie,

"It's time to decide,
what you're doing, how you're going to reach your way.
It's time to decide,
a day tomorrow just might be too late."

45

Come Hold Restless Ideas Seen Together

You've been so long in my corner.
I've watched you so carefully, though patiently,
I've watched my needs grow.

Words seem to hide when I need you;
they're lost in my pocket somewhere.
I search desperately, but it's all uselessly.

But I'm losing my mind in your eyes;
I'm holding a dream in my heart.
I'd like to share it but I just can't say it,
well enough.

But I've been so long in your corner,
I knew your love someday might shine on me;
on me, so patiently, I've watched my needs grow.
Come hold restless ideas seen together.

46

Over And Done

Over, after it's all said and done,
after the words are just dealings,
they lose their feelings and concerns.
Over, with a love that was second to none,
a love that passion carried,
although now varied, still burns.
Over, confused and perplexed,
wondering what to do next;
no warm heart waiting for anyone,
and a love that's over and done, and a love,...
Questions, only emphasize all of the doubt,
with no answers for all of the ranges
of the changes we now face.
Reasons, hard to say what things were about;
it's too late for speculation, with relations out of place.
Over, no kiss or embrace,
and I'm so lonely here without Grace;
an empty heart watching a setting sun,
as a love is over and done; as a love,...
is over and done,...

47

Where Is The Love?
(Bulldozer)

The skyline's taking no time to break the ground it's on,
but it seems my sorrow lies
with the woods and forests gone.

And where is the love? Oh, where is the love?
All the love they promised,
all the love we all needed,
the love...?

Two schools and three hundred houses
got to go for this freeway.
Everywhere behind a dump
or a road leading away.

But where is the love? Oh, where is the love?
All the love they promised,
all the love we all needed,
the love...?

48

Fairfax After Midnight

Snow,...
wind blow,
gray clouds in the sky,
goodnight with a sigh,
goodnight
goodbye.
No pain,...
lost in frozen rain,
and a thundering sky.
Goodnight with a sigh,
goodnight
goodbye.
No sight,...
all is night.
Don't you wonder why
all good things must die?
Goodnight with a sigh,
goodnight
goodbye,...
Goodbye.

49

Song For The Road

Here is a song for the road; may it carry your load.
Help you fly if you've a care,
and safely bring you down when you get there.

And believe this road is hard,
with repairs in need for a road so marred.
But your song will not be gone, and your road will lead you on.

May you see through eyes of youth; may you finally find your truth.
May that truth help to set you free,
and may your road lead you safely home to me.

And believe this road is hard,
with repairs in need for a road so marred.
But your song will not be gone, and the road will lead you on.

May you see through eyes of youth, may you finally find your truth.
May that truth help to set you free,
and may your road lead you safely home to me.

50

MEMOIRS & NOTES - 24 -
'NEW SUITS'

New Suits

(1993) – In 1992, after a falling away, I watched two people that I loved dearly go through a divorce. At first there was a good sense of calm civility and respect for each other, but it escalated into an intense and ugly confrontation as their children divided into different camps and money or the distribution thereof became the underlying and final issue that totally put an end to the whole relationship.

In the end, because money was the chief instigation or fuel for the vindictive fire, it is no surprise that lawyers got involved to straighten things out. From the insistence of the lawyers, there was a terrible battle in court, which  left both of my friends emotionally devastated. And it is no surprise that after the finalization of the proceedings, the only ones that truly benefited from the divorce was both of the lawyers from either side.

Interestingly enough, the two lawyers that faced off for this litigation were good friends and ultimately held no malice between each other or their clients.

Wall Street is a street located in the lower Manhattan section of New York City and is the home of the New York Stock Exchange or NYSE. Wall Street has also been the historic headquarters of some of the largest U.S. brokerages and investment banks.

A stockbroker is a professional trader who buys and sells shares on behalf of clients. The stockbroker may also be known as a registered representative or an investment advisor. Most stockbrokers work for a brokerage firm and handle transactions for a number of individual and institutional customers.

But stockbrokers can get greedy,... Their Crimes are simple: *the stockbroker steals the client's money*, and they can do that in many ways. Stockbrokers have been known to steal client funds by simply forging letters of authorization, directing that funds be transferred from the customer account to another account controlled by the broker. In other cases, brokers have established phantom accounts at other institutions where the broker is shown as a joint account holder, and which is used as a depository for funds siphoned out of the customer's actual account, which then the broker simply steals. Sometimes to conceal these withdrawals, a broker may change the customer's address, diverting the actual statements from ever reaching the customer, and then manufacture their own phony statements to send to the customer instead.

Like plastic on plastic where there is a strong sense of hopelessness due to the inability to control things, the whole system, with its checks and balances, for and of protective law, seems out of reach to the common man. There is no doubt that in the criminal justice system, they are the ones in full control. They know all the ins and outs to every crime known to man. And if you get put in a questionable circumstance, know that the more you pay does not guarantee better service.

And lawyers are, (and have been for centuries), a necessary evil; keeping the criminals controlled. and they permeate everything from our pharmaceuticals to our groceries, to the health care system, to the music industry; hailing everywhere from our smallest of towns to the corrupt politics of the legislature in Washington D.C. And who ultimately watches the watchmen of law? Meanwhile the people in the legal profession that work for us, the new suits that we pay to help us maintain some control in our lives, they—the new suits are the ones really in control. Here's a fun fact; there are even lawyers out here that specialize in defending other lawyers.

Side Note:

And then there's lobbyists and special interest groups; most all of which are or have been lawyers. Lobbyists are professionals hired by special interest groups to represent whatever their interests are, to Congress. The very nature of lobbying deals with attempting to influence decisions made by a public official — usually to pass or defeat legislation. All kinds of groups hire lobbyists — from corporations and private companies to nonprofits and unions, all trying to persuade the government to pass legislation that will be favorable, to them. The problem materializes when lobbyists use money to buy influence with our government. Lobbyists funnel millions of dollars into the hands of Congress, and because they've become dependent on money from lobbyists to fund their political careers, Congress ends up passing laws to keep the lobbyists and their clients happy, instead of laws that benefit the American people.

Another Side Note:

Seven months after I wrote this song the OJ Simpson fiasco began and the whole country saw the world of high-profile lawyers, fighting against and with each other, at their mind-game calculatingly best, and dishonest, vicious, back-stabbing worst.

Simpson was represented by a high-profile defense team, also referred to as the "Dream Team", which was initially led by Robert Shapiro and subsequently directed by Johnnie Cochran. The team also included F.

Lee Bailey, Alan Dershowitz, Robert Kardashian, Shawn Holley, Carl E. Douglas, and Gerald Uelmen. Barry Scheck and Peter Neufeld were two additional attorneys who specialized in DNA evidence.

Deputy District Attorneys Marcia Clark, William Hodgman and later Christopher Darden thought that they had a strong case against Simpson, but Cochran was able to convince the jury that there was reasonable doubt concerning the validity of the State's DNA evidence, which was a relatively new form of evidence in trials at that time. The reasonable doubt theory included evidence that the blood sample had allegedly been mishandled by lab scientists and technicians, and there were questionable circumstances that surrounded other court exhibits.

Cochran and the defense team also alleged other misconduct by the LAPD related to systemic racism and incompetence, in particular actions and comments of Detective Mark Fuhrman who, when asked under oath whether he had planted or manufactured evidence in the case, invoked his Fifth Amendment right and declined to answer. According to the defense, this raised the possibility that Fuhrman had planted key evidence as part of a racially motivated plot against Simpson. An audiotape proving that Fuhrman perjured himself and thereby undermining the credibility of the prosecution has been cited as one reason Simpson was acquitted.

Johnnie Cochran, the lead defense attorney earned up to $5 million from helping to win Simpson's acquittal on double murder charges. Given that during the trial, Simpson was represented by at least 10 attorneys, if you do the math ($500,000 x 10), you get an estimate of about $5 million.

But Simpson's legal bill is insignificant compared to what the prosecution spent for their case — almost double. It is estimated that the prosecution's case against Simpson cost taxpayers a whopping $9 million. This number includes the cost of district attorney Marcia

Clark, assistant attorneys William Hodgman and Christopher Darden, the court costs (judge, court reporters, judicial assistants), sequestering of jury, the sheriff's deputies providing security, and the cost of Simpson's incarceration for 473 days.

In 1997, Marcia Clark published her own tell-all about the case for which she earned a reported $4.2 million, unfortunately, she was unable to change the story line or outcome, but you can buy a lot of comfort food with that much money.

It's Too Late

(1993) – My big mistake was to live and exist in this black and white world and dream in color. We are what we do and what we say and how we interact with others and all of our mistakes and shortcomings, besides the opportunities to learn from, are all parts of the "baggage" we carry with us on the journey. So many ideas and possibilities; the dreams that we carry with us to shore up and hide our, currently sad circumstances; but as those wonderful, sumptuous dreams dissolve in front of us, leaving us standing, exposed to the naked truth of our menial existence, we may slump into a heartbreaking heap or choose new directions. We may even determine, that sometime later, we will rise above our current circumstances and become or do or see or experience that other side, or perspective. Those things that we see others possess, things that we try not to covet, they call to us and mock our inability to gain such, but we just know in God's graces that we deserve such things too; but after a long wait, and when it still never happens, we become even more frustrated or disillusioned with the whole process.

And then there's the perspective of being the good family guy, soldiering on, dealing with one problem after another, all with a hopeful disposition as we carry the hopes of a better tomorrow. And tomorrow keeps getting push back and delayed until it becomes obvious that tomorrow never comes. But to eke out our passions and dreams at the expense of someone else's misfortune would seem, well it's not me and I've had enough experiences where friends and others have used me or taken advantage of our relationship, for their preverbal climb up their steps towards success, all at the expense of my expended time, energy or money; leading to that separation of trust and or friendship; I can't do that, I won't do that.

I want my children to have all the best things in life even to the point of self-denial, but I can only do so much with what I have and then hope to be blessed with the other things that we might need to be getting by.

Side Note:

Living the lie that things will get better in the future and then we'll have time for all the things that we missed or couldn't afford along the way is a slippery slope. Hey, it is all just a lie, and I'm not advocating the "eat drink, be merry for tomorrow we die" philosophy, but I think we do need to open our eyes today, look for the love aimed at us, and the opportunity to reach out to give our love to others; to live and love like there will be no tomorrow.

A Long Way To Go

(1992) – We all have this time to spend here on earth; some have only a few moments while others spend over a century, but we have all been gifted with this thing called life and free agency to do what we think is important. It seems that many of us take a lot of time trying to figure out what life is all about, while others seem to hit the ground running as they maximize their time and accomplish great things. Either way, as Jim Morrison reported in the Door's song, "Five To One," that, "no one here gets out alive;" we are all ultimately heading down a one-way street that has an ending somewhere down that road.

It took me too long to realize that even though we are all on that road going at separate paces and strides, but something many lose focus on and important to note, we are not racing each other. We may think that we are, and in fact, competitively, we may feel good when we stretch ahead of others, or sad when we seem to fall behind others, (does this sound familiar to you?) but that is, for too many, some false gauge to be used or even pushed out by those who need justification for their worldly pursuits of money or power or fame, and if you didn't accept their terms of engagement into that race, you're made to feel inferior by comparison, but also, for the competitors, there would be no way for them to measure their success. Trying to make sense of the whole life thing going on all around us can be disheartening.

Philosophically, and from other perspectives, this doesn't mean that people should stop striving to do their best, but it does mean that we are all in this pursuit of measuring our progress from one moment to another, with ourselves. But we can never measure progress from one point to another or know how we're doing in life if we don't know where we are, progress wise from one moment to another. This song was an attempt to lay down this viewpoint or way of thinking. I still don't have it all figured out, but I'm still on this journey with a long way to go.

Side Note:

When I was ten, I had a problem, (maybe more on this later), and had to go to the hospital and have an emergency operation to get circumcised. When I was given ether by the anesthesiologist, I remember him talking to me as I was supposed to be going to sleep, and then, although I should have been out, I could hear the anesthesiologist say to one of the nurses that it didn't look like I was breathing. The next thing I remember was I was looking down at the operating table as the anesthesiologist was scurrying to give me oxygen and other doctors were arriving to see what was going on, and then I seemed to drift somewhere else, floating on some circular path, that in a wheel-like motion like a merry-go-round, kept returning to the starting point, and then I fell asleep and woke up after the operation. Maybe it was the ether, maybe it was something else, but that story has stayed with me and has caused me to consider and or wonder about the meaning of my life.

Time To Decide

(1981) – Didn't write too much in 1981 because I lacked the inspiration; I didn't feel good about myself, where I was going, or ultimately what I was doing. I've had my time sitting on the fence and wondering which side I ought to settle on, choose and jump down into or onto one side or the other.

Many years had passed since I stopped turning on and had either I lost track or fell out of favor with most of my old buddies, and I vacillated over whether or not I should slide a bit and take comfort there again. But my fifth child, Ben had just been born and the reasons for me leaving that Arena all came back to me and I let those ideas of breaking the word of wisdom go by the way.

From the late 60s, my friend Louie never changed. Except for an occasional temp job here and there, he continued to live mostly off of the dope (smoke) he sold which paid for his rent, his food and his head. He never found any higher purpose in life than to get stoned and have good time. At one time I envy him and his lifestyle, but as years went by and my posterity began to increase, I only felt sorrier for him. This song was not completely about him per se, but more so, it was about the fact that we all are walking on this thin fence ready to fall either direction at any moment and knowing that if it's not a choice, it could very well be the wrong side.

Side Note:

We had some good friends and neighbors across the street called the Pisanos, (Danny and Rita). Rita with all her younger kids, and Diane with all of our younger kids, were thick as thieves and shared good company with each other, trading off who's house they'd meet at almost every day.

Rita, amongst other things, was a midwife in training, and of course, with the advent of a baby arriving any day to our house, Diane was talked into having Rita deliver the baby. This was an exciting time for Diane because she's read about this midwifery thing and felt it was the right thing to do. The time for it to happen came late on a, more than warm, August fifth night. Rita was right there, taking vital signs, checking dilations, taking control. I think because Rita felt the anxious vibes in the air, (probably mostly from me), she started monologuing things softly as she flittered around the room, getting everything ready. She would be checking Diane out and saying things like, "So what we're gonna see here is that the first stage of labor and birth occurs when Diane begins to feel regular contractions, which will cause the cervix to dilate,..." And then moving over to take Diane's temperature she would add, "and soften, shorten and the thinning of the cervix, which is measured in percentages." Sensing that I'm starting to get nervous, she says calmly, "You got nothing to worry about here, this process called effacement allows the baby to move into the birth canal." I nodded like I understood but by now, Diane was starting to make weird, uncomfortable noises and I was getting even more anxious. Rita directed me to sit on the bed behind Diane with my back to the wall and I was supposed to massage Diane to keep her calm and to somehow keep me connected to the whole process. As I get there in position, Rita says, "The cervix must be 100 percent effaced and 10 centimeters dilated before a good delivery."

And now I didn't care any more about what Rita was saying because Diane began moaning even louder. I reached over from behind her and started to caress her shoulders when she yelled out at me in a very angry tone for me to stop touching her. Meanwhile I'm now locked in behind Diane and there was no way to get out from behind her, and therefore, no way to stop touching her.

Rita, who was standing in delivery position reached in and took a measurement then placed her fingers on a cardboard chart before she excitedly called out, "We got eight centimeters here folks."

"What,..." I began to ask but was interrupted by Diane who yelled emphatically, "Chester, Stop talking!"

"It's okay, it's okay." Rita said apologetically to me.

Another loud unintelligible outburst came from Diane as Rita took position and Ben came out to see what was happening. I took the opportunity to escape my prison. Maybe seeing the disappointment on my face from being trapped behind the mad woman, or maybe from me not being able to watch the delivery of my son, Rita handed me a pair of scissors and told me that I could cut the ambilocal chord.

"She probably won't remember being so unpleasant to you." Rita said to me on the side after handing the swaddled baby to Diane. "This happens all the time."

It did take me a while to get over seeing and being treated by Diane like that, and weeks later when I did bring it up, Diane categorically denied speaking and treating me in such a fashion.

Come Hold Restless Ideas Seen Together

(1971) – After writing the words to this song down on a small, four by seven-inch paper, and then playing with it by adding various chord progressions to it, I was indifferent. At the time, the essence of the song seemed rather trite, or lacking in substance, along with my scattered train of thought to the words of the song, and like many other songs back then, I threw it away. Diane pulled the small piece of paper out of the trashcan and sometime later, told me that she liked this one. So, I went back to the drawing board (so to speak), and rewrote the tune to more closely follow the feel of the words, and this was a result. It is always nice to have someone that believes in you, and I have to say that Diane was ultimately my inspiration and continues to be so to this day.

Side Note:

This song means so much more now that we've been married for all these years, and singing it, brings me back to that time when it was written but also follows me into today and tomorrow. My needs for her have evolved and still continues to grow, and it brings to home the fact that, although her needs and my needs have changed over time, the essence of the truths inside the words to this song still ring clearly in my mind and in my heart.

Over And Done

(1993) – The words to this song came out of some guitar chords I was strumming late one night and the idea of a love being over and done materialized, and ultimately, dominated the theme to this song. This is another one of those songs that I envisioned in my mind going a certain direction only to end up somewhere else. Originally, because the subject matter reflected a breakup with him knowing it was really over and done, I was going with a lot more minor chords along with a running structure of G to Em woven through the piece. But the end result I got from recording this song was still very pleasing to me and so this was the results. Someday I hope to rerecord this song and maybe capture what I had heard that night while strumming those other chords to this song.

Side Note:

Not long after the trauma and shock of the **Second** BIG HURT, (my brother David getting kicked out of the house), I started having problems in school with organizational skills, I couldn't seem to focus or prioritize my daily tasks. So fearful that I would be the next David to Senior, I was always diligent in keeping distance between me and him, but it came at a cost of endless restlessness and constant edginess, even when I was safely in my bed trying to go to sleep. With all my energies concentrated on survival, other things began to happen, like I would constantly forget things, like doing my homework, and I kept losing things in class, like pencils or pencil sharpeners or even books seemed to disappear from my desk. I had a variable lack of attention that would get me in trouble, but after a while, I didn't care about that anymore. There was a lot of stress just trying to fit in to my circumstances, but if my full attention was needed to continue to exist, who cares about how well I could write my name in cursive? (And that was a really big deal in Catholic schools).

But then I developed a new problem that would bring me even more grief; nocturnal enuresis or in other words, wetting my bed. My mother was sympathetic to my circumstances and wanted to work with me on it, but when Senior found out, he knew that the only solution, at least from the perspective of his Italian father who was from the old Sicilian country, was a good old-fashioned spanking. And not just a few warning slaps on my rear end in passing, he liked to pull all my clothes off and make solid noticeable connections with a strong hand (or belt) to my bare bottom.

That only happened a few times, because after that, I was careful not to drink anything after dinner, and although I was mighty thirsty at times, I hardly ever did. Mother also came to my rescue and gave me a stack of my baby sister Mary's diapers, and instructed me to pad myself in the front with as many as I could fit under my underwear. She also moved the diaper pail from her room next to the crib to a place outside the kitchen by the back porch, so in the morning I could then take all of the urine-soaked diapers and put them covertly and directly into the diaper pail where Mary's dirty diapers were.

Knowing I was now on Senior's radar, (something I had been trying to avoid), and knowing that he was checking up on me with my mother to see if I'd had an recent accidents, I conveniently stopped using sheets altogether, putting them over to one side, and instead, I had an army blanket wrapped around me. And in the morning, I would stash the army blanket in my closet behind to my wicker hamper that housed my comic books and treasures and I would put the sheets back in place.

It didn't happen as fast as I'd have liked it to, but I did get past this obstacle and again worked hard at being invisible to Senior.

Bulldozer (Where Is The Love?)

(1970) – This song is about the seemingly heartless and unkind demeanor of any city, county and state commissioner in charge of building new roads at the expense of, and the cheating theft thereof of the common homeowner, who has no recourse or choice but to move and accept the paltry amounts given.

Grandma Scarbrough lived in a wonderful neighborhood in South East Portland Oregon for 34 years, until one day the state decided to move forward with the creation of the 37 miles (60 km) long, Interstate 205, (I-205), (also known as the East Portland Freeway No. 64).

Side Note:

This freeway was to be an auxiliary Interstate Highway in the Portland metropolitan area of Oregon and Washington and would serve as a bypass route of I-5, traveling north–south along the east side of Portland, Oregon, and Vancouver, Washington, intersecting several major highways and serving a quicker way to access the Portland International Airport. 205 ran from the South East end of Vancouver Washington, across Government Island, and then through South East Portland all the way to Oregon City.

Another Side Note:

Grandma's house, along with two schools and over 300 other houses, (not to mention the hundreds of businesses, gas stations and shops) were all taken out for the building of this freeway. Unfortunately, as mentioned in another song, ("A Hole In The Sky" from the "Ever On" album), her house and her three lots ended up as part of the north-bound Foster Road

Grandma Scarbrough's House on 96th Street

off ramp in the Lents District. Although the freeway had begun in 1964, the big push, especially in the Lents District, happened in 1970 and my grandma Scarbrough was forced to move to another home maybe a mile away. I was not too long after her having to deal with the trauma and anxiety of having to lose her property after intense pressure was enforced by the city, and I still feel that the hassle of it all affected her deeply and she got sick, never recovered, and passed away on November 28, 1973.

Fairfax After Midnight

(1970-71) – This is another one of my early guitar songs and was written perhaps in 1970, after I got settled in Portland, and more likely revised and finished in 1971 while I was staying at the Kingston Apartments

that from my second-story window, overlooked a stadium to the left and a large parking lot to the right, both of which had been covered with snow. As I looked out onto the scene, it all seemed so quiet and peaceful and yet in some remote way, it seemed dis-turbingly ominous and foreboding. With this mixed emotional setting going on in my head, I sat on the bed and recited words as I played some spooky chords. Even though I was infatuated with these dark, wonderful chords I walked down the hall to talk with George and when I got back the music had left. After struggling to regain the progression, I gave up, took the words and put different chords to it, making it suddenly different as it took on a different personification that reminded me of "Deep Purple."

The lyrics to this song reflect the coming and nurturing of a good dream that carries the hope of tomorrow, like the way I felt in one night in Hollywood in the summer of 1967. I was standing outside of Canter's Delicatessen, Bakery, Restaurant, (open 24 hours), at two in the morning with my friend Tim Sappington, surrounded by dozens of heads and believers; some congregating in and out of Canter's, others drift-

ing up and down Fairfax, looking for acceptance or drift over to and through the Headshop on the corner a block away – also open 24 hours. It was a time of spiritual enlightenment, a path to the promised land of insight and illumination of the soul for those on a search for meaning and purpose. But it was also so transitory; a time of fleeting illusions, short-lived or even conflicting information and differing explanations, ephemeral fantasies that many were buying into, that, like the high they were on, faded hours later leaving the remains of whatever their true reality was, to contemplate as they ventured back to what homes that had at the time. It was glorious in its moment, but was also a sadness, as the realization that the dream will never reach fruition and will fade away like the soiled winter snow melting on a warm spring afternoon.

Side Note:

One late night, early morning, after I had gotten off work from Burger Chef, I played this song over at Louie's apartment. It was well received but he said he didn't get it and asked me what it was all about. I told him it was about the fleeting hippy movement during a time in the 60s. He asked me to play it again, which I did, and when I finished, Louie turned to me and smiling, said, "I still don't get it."

Calm Down - All This Heat (Instrumental)

(1993) – This is a short clip, (1:53) of the complete instrumental that came out on the album, "On The Edge Of A Very Strange Light," completed in 1994. Technically, both pieces are a combination of two separate pieces; "Calm Down," and, "All This Heat." And if you listen carefully and kind of sing along to the music, you can maybe hear where I was going to put words to each; "Calm down" was the first part, and just a few seconds past the middle of this rendition, "All This Heat" comes in till the end where "Calm Down" fades in and out to end this rendition. Yes, there was a draft of words to go with this piece but it was discarded in favor of what was ended up with, and I have never found those drafts, but I can always recreate things if I feel like it later on.

Song For The Road

(1972) – By the time I wrote this song in 1972, Diane and I were unofficially, boyfriend—girlfriend. Out and about, I was doing mini performances for friends and family or whenever or wherever the occasion happened, and I would play on until I ran out of polished material; which was about 60 minutes, but, unless I felt some great interest in my material, (which hardly ever happened), I would keep it down to about 30 minutes. And as I was packing it up, I would almost always seem to hear someone say, "How about if you play one more song for the road?"

This was my motivation to writing this song; and then as a goof, as someone asked, "How about one more song for the road?" I would not only play a last song, but I would play this song; "Song For The Road." It was a good joke that many got a laugh over, at first, but after hearing the song; a thoughtful piece that reflected hopefulness for an uncertain future, the song was usually met with good appraisal.

We are all out there "on the road" to wherever, from wherever, for whatever reasons; it's hard enough getting from one place to another without encountering obstacles in our path that, even for a given moment of our precious time, impede our progress or temporarily keep us from our given destinations. It is comforting to know that we don't have to be out there on that road alone; that there is always someone that waits for our return, that commiserates with our problems and setbacks, someone that loves us. As I would have others rally round my cause and needs, I have taken it upon myself to try to be that someone for another out there in need. And that road out there can be hard for someone already having other issues, and it's my hope to be sensitive enough to be of help when I can.

Side Note:

Originally, this was written for piano, but at that time I had no piano to practice with and so, it gravitated to guitar. And when I recorded the song eleven years later, I played with both, but I felt like the guitar really held the interest more; and so it goes. I did have a soft #12 organ background that complimented the rhythm harmonica at the end of the song.

Another Side Note:

As maybe mentioned before, I was not highly favored by Diane's roommates, even though we'd been together for a while, and in fact, met up with repeated skepticism for my desires to get involved in the music business. This was especially true with Sally, who never missed a chance to throw in a dig whenever she felt the opportunity was ripe. But this was the first song that she did not have a critic for. Arguably it has a nice tune, with optimism and thoughtful lyrics of anticipation for a promising tomorrow; she didn't say anything and I watched her face as she moved to another room. Her face said something like, "I wish there was something I could say negative about that song, but I can't." More on this development later in notes on the, "City Boy" album.

❧

- 25 - LISTENING TO THE NEWS - 1993 -

NOTES ABOUT THE COVERS

Note s On The New Cover:

All of my copies of the original cover were corrupt. I thought about doing a whole new cover, but I was in a hurry to get my stuff published and this cover ended up being the results of something I cobbled together.

Notes On The Original Covers:

First, let me say that the original to this cover was hard to find. Second, you may see that the original cover is cleaner than the new cover; for good reason.

Microsoft File Manager is terrible for searching, but after downloading a program called *"Everything,"* I found the original cover, which was a creation of my own where I took the dash of an old vehicle and cut the beach scene to fit in the window. The back cover was part of a project I was doing for Bill Bragg and Yesterday USA.

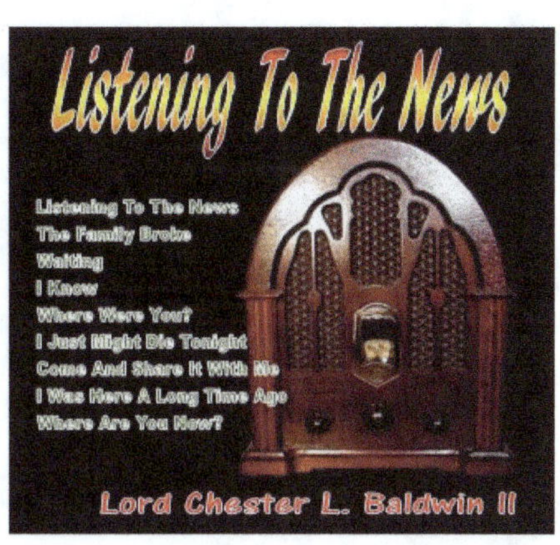

53

LISTENING TO THE NEWS

Listening To The News
The Family Broke
Waiting
I Know
Where Were You?
I Just Might Die Tonight
Come And Share It With Me
I Was Here A Long Time Ago
Where Are You Now?

54

Listening To The News

I got a long way to drive to work each day,
so, I turn on the radio, to hear what's happening today.
There's a coup and a revolt breaking through the city walls,
as some little army wins and some little country falls.
I know someone's got to win and somebody's got to lose,
but I'm just driving down the road; listening to the news.

They found these barrels that were dumped by the sound,
that's killing off the plant life and poisoning the ground.
A nuclear plant story, renews concerns and fears,
we ain't really as safe as they've been saying all these years.
In my mind, I just imagine, all that radioactive ooze,
as I'm driving down the road; listening to the news.

Incest, rape and murder with corruption of all sorts,
are sprinkled with interludes of the weather and the sports.
People trying to change the world, the wrongs to be trued,
are being restricted, penalized or maybe just misconstrued.
Thinking how I might feel stepping in their shoes,
driving down the road; listening to the news.

Justice and injustice from the crime scene to the courts,
well I'm hoping for something good
to come out of all these reports.
But I just hear about people killing for money,
or because they're in the mood,
and there's people in some third world
that are starving without food.
I got this uneasy feeling like the empty pocket blues,
cause I'm driving down the road, listening to the news.

The top story tonight repeats again and again,
as there is no beginning and there is no end.
It's a battle for the ratings and the audience within,
as they market misery, deprivation and sin.
The solutions to regain balance? No one has a clue,
we're all just driving down the road, listening to the news.

55

The Family Broke

We used to feed each other's hopes,
helped the young to learn the ropes.
Those were the trusting, good old days,
now we've gone our separate ways.
Not like the slamming of the door,
it was a growing sickness more,
that year; the family broke.

What's to say of the real life
for the parents that won't try?
They stopped working for a cause meant well,
and they could only see themselves.
Went to sleep in separate beds,
thinking out of separate heads,
and so; the family broke.

We as children didn't understand
what motivates or breaks the plan.
We were forced to choose a side;
Father, Mother, no "Un-Decides."

Though my heart burned and ached,
I never showed it on my face,
that day; the family broke.

Years have passed, all here and there,
I'm still not going anywhere.
Though the parents felt no other course,
still had no reasons for divorce.
All the children, scattered along,
some still searching for what is home
like before; the family broke.

56

Waiting

She took my money, and she took the car,
she took the kids, and there you are.
And I'm waiting, waiting for her to come home.
She emptied our account and got on a train,
but I don't know if she's coming back again,
but I'm waiting, waiting for her to come home.
She emptied the house, left it in a mess,
but she didn't leave any forward address,
so I'm waiting, waiting for her to come home.
I sit around the house, watching T.V.
staring out the window in disbelief
and I'm waiting,
yeah, I'm waiting for her to come home.
She made me think, and I'm beginning to see,
the impact she had on my life, and me,
and I'm waiting, waiting for her to come home.
She still ain't called, I'm beginning to fear
she'll never know I need her back here;
and I'm waiting, waiting for her to come home.

57

I Know

You don't have to go anywhere,
say a word, or do anything
because I know; I know.
You won't need a social degree,
in psychology to speak to me
because I know; I know.
All the values no one seems to use
they haven't changed and neither should you.
You don't have to try to hide,
pretend you're happy while you're torn up inside
because I know; I know.
The thoughts and feelings you're going through,
I went through those changes just like you,
and I know; I know.
A little truth will tear down the lies,
as you open your heart and open your eyes.
You don't have to be on your own,
with one good friend, you're never alone,
and I know; I know.
I know; I know.

58

Where Were You?

Where were you when the troubles all began;
I needed you to lean on now and then?
Where were you when the bank threatened their plan
and we had to move to trailer town again?

Where were you when everything fell all apart
and I couldn't think where to go or what to do?
When I was trying to recover from a broken heart,
and I needed love; where were you?

Where were you when the old septic system froze,
and everything backed up, nothing would perk?
Where were you when that stupid, old car broke,
and I had to walk ten miles, out to work?

Where were you when I was lost, alone in the dark,
and didn't know where to go or what to do?
When I was trying to recover from a broken heart,
and I needed love; where were you?

Where were you when the bills all arrived?
Where were you when the checkbook took a dive?
And where were you when the kids were all sad?
And where were you when I needed you so bad?

Where were you when the new day awoke,
and I needed someone to comfort me?
Where were you as that long weekend broke
and I was home alone with kids watching T.V.?

Where were you when everything fell all apart
and I couldn't think where to go or what to do?
When I was trying to recover from this broken heart,
and I needed love, where were you?

When I was trying to recover from this broken heart,
and I needed love, where were you?

59

I Just Might Die Tonight

Though time is moving fast, my mind is in the past.
I look to see the world,
and it's dangled and it's swirled,
and knowing I am right,
I just might die tonight, I just might die tonight.

For something I don't regret. For something I can't regret.
Something inside me told me I was right.
and as I'm sitting here, I think,
that I just might die tonight, I just might die tonight.

Too many people don't care if they're going anywhere,
but the worst, that is the sin;
they have nothing to believe in.
But I stood by what I believed was right
and as I'm sitting here I feel,
I just might die tonight, I just might die tonight.

Come And Share It With Me

I've been thinking in this fog,
I'm just a silhouette in all this smog,
but I refuse to be a hog,
so come and share it with me.
All my tree friends from within
are rapidly losing all their kin.
But kill for sport you mighty men,
and come and share it with me.
Powers raging for an ultimate gain,
peons starving in the cold hard rain.
Your glory rots on slated graves
so come and share it with me.
Nothing here can seem to grow,
tumbleweeds roll as the prairie winds blow,
and the dollar died a year ago;
come and share it with me.
Destroy your truths and forget your fears,
don't worry about your way out of here.
With any luck, we'll make next year,
so come and share it with me.

61

I Was Here A Long Time Ago

I was here a long time ago.
I saw the angels come and I saw the angels go.
And I remember you singing in that grand parade,
Excited and yet hopeful for all the glory made.
I was here a long time ago.
I saw the mountains high and the valleys below.
We all cheered the making and the possibilities;
the glory of creation for all humanities.
I was here a long time ago.
A new land full of promise; generations to grow.
All the rights and wrongs were weighted out with care
were upon the chosen people and everybody there.
I was here a long time ago. Yet sometime I stopped viewing
when came my time to go.
I knew all yet forgot as my turn soon came near,
and now I'm so confused over why I'm really here.
I was here a long time ago.
I can't seem to remember what it is that I should know.
Where I came from, why I'm here, or where I should go,
relates to when I was here a long time ago.

62

Where Are You Now?

We never said goodbye, but it was well implied to me,
when we just stopped talking of the future
and we lost all our common dreams.
I was standing outside your porch
as your mother said you weren't at home;
I caught a glimpse of you turned the other way
talking on the telephone.
It took me years to get over all the hang-ups I had from you.
All my plans were changed and the detours made,
as I searched for something new,
and I just kept on looking for that letter or call
that never did arrive.
And the special thing that we had long ago,
only dissolved with time.
Those years ago, and happenings will never come back again.
It's much too late to regret the past
and all the might-have-beens.
Everything seemed so complicated and hard,
and we just couldn't see how.
Still, I wonder at times as I think of us, where are you now?

63

࿇

MEMOIRS & NOTES - 25 - 'LISTENING TO THE NEWS'

Listening To The News

(1993) – By the time this album was completed I was on a roll, and because I had this repertoire of material that went back 20 years, I was recording something new almost every night. Even more so, I was writing new material too, and then sandwiching them in-between my older material. Good times. Well, it was still a lot of work.

I am a big fan of commercial-free Public News Radio, (NPR), and would listen to it faithfully, but every three months they would have these incessant pledge drives that solicit my financial support while interrupting or preempting the stories, spoiling the ambiance

Listening To The News On The Radio in A 1967 Chevy-Nova

of the news stories' taking as much time as a commercial to thank

193

benefactors, and in doing so, they become an ongoing collection of commercials themselves.

It was during one of these pledge weeks that I reverted to local news on the AM stations. The differences are stark and noticeable from their attempt to power-hit only on the mainstream news, to the minimal coverage of every story in 15 seconds or less, to the interpretation of the story by the producers or the owners that want to push their own secret or not so secret agenda. And sometimes it just seems that we're all inundated with too much information.

Like television, these radio news stories are tightly structured, although rather disconnected one from the other, presented in modules that are always predictable and consistently reused. In fact, I could turn on a different station to find that they are both simultaneously reporting the local then national sports or having an update to the road reports or having commercials.

But the main essence of what this song documents is the station's inability to be personal as they find themselves in alienation with their own public, due to their sponsor's control, and the station's own inability for true compassion for the listeners or the people in their coverage; as they quickly touch on sensationalistic stories of assumed incest, then quickly move ahead to a story about a dog that was killed in a house fire, then a story of an attempted rape and then on to a possible ambiguous murder in some close bedroom community and then after five to ten minutes of commercials they follow up with sports, weather and a traffic report.

I gained a stronger respect for NPR and sometimes I even tolerate their pledge drives just to avoid the unpleasant alternative, sometimes. Sometimes silence is far better.

Side Note:

Tutsi soldiers after the 1993 elections in the
Republic of Burundi

In the 1993 elections, Melchior Ndadaye, a Hutu, defeated Buyoya to win the nation's first free presidential election. Soon afterward he was overthrown and killed in a coup attempt by Tutsi soldiers. The Republic of Burundi was convulsed by ethnic violence in which thousands of Hutus and Tutsis died, and many fled the country.

Also, in the spring of 1993, barrels of waste, (radioactive waste?) were found, dumped in the Puget Sound area. It was speculated that they came from Hanford but I never heard a follow up to the story ever appear.

Another Side Note:

Ah yes, birthdays. And Liz turned the golden age of 16 in 1993. Now a couple years earlier maybe three years prior, I stressed out on what to give her for her birthday. 12 or 13 or 14 or even 15-year-old boys were always easy; in those days video games were becoming desirable but a bike was always at the top of their lists followed by other moving things like, a bb gun, (which Diane did not allow), a frisbee or a football or a basketball or some other sports thing, and then maybe follow that up with their favorite candy bar and a box of their favorite cereal. But girls or at least my girls didn't want those things which I found out when Liz turned 13. Which, by the way, happens right when school starts, and did I mention that I was an eleven-month employee at SPSCC with no money coming in till the middle of October?

It's such an odd age, 13, made even more odd because 13-year-old girls don't even like what other 13-year-old girls like let alone what 13-year-old boys like. And a girl's maturity level is different than a boy's, as I found out that year. First, I brought home a red-rubber playground ball, you know the kind you play four square or dodge ball with. I know

I still love them. they bounce well, you can kick them to the moon and it never hurts your feet like footballs do when you kick them wrong.

At the time, nylons were popular and they didn't last very well, so I got her one of those big eggs with a pair of panty hose inside. I got her an inexpensive but good-toned harmonica, an orange sweatshirt with a hood, (it was on sale), a box of her favorite cereal and a candy bar (Snickers), and called it good. Birthday cake comes out, she blows out the candles and then the gifts arrive, as Christopher, two, wants to be in charge of the bag of presents. As Liz starts opening the presents, with the help of Spencer and Christopher, she does not look excited; moreover, she looks mildly upset. When the playground ball gets opened, and although Christopher loved it, I suddenly realized that Liz is looking around for that other gift, the one that's probably hiding somewhere. When she comes to the realization that this is it, she starts crying and runs into her room to be alone.

The following year she's 14 and besides a box of her favorite cereal and a candy bar I got her a dress from Mervin's (that was on sale); too small. Next year I got her the usuals, and some art supplies, which I gotta say, she did like, and I don't know what possessed me, but I bought her a jet-black bra. Not only did I get chastised for the color of the bra, (it was on sale), but the cups were so big that Meridith put it on her head and was wearing it for a hat. For years that story has been perpetuated and passed on like I would need to have to remember what not to get girls for their birthdays or Christmas.

Ah yes, birthdays. And Liz turned the golden age of 16. That year I got smart; I gave whatever money I had socked away to Diane and told her it was her turn. I don't honestly know what she gave her, and maybe that says something in and of itself.

Yet Another Side Note:

As a delivery driver in the mid-70s and again in the mid-80s, I consumed a lot of talk radio. I used to scramble at times just to be able to listen to Paul Harvey when he came on at noon or 3:30 in the afternoon. And there were other favorite people to listen to, and they mostly made sense, and they collectively were non-bias and they were fun to interact with. Of late it seems everyone has an agenda and a need to be recognized with a brand and a one-sided agenda to preach. Not a fan. Democrat-centered radio shows spewing disrespect for the bombastic republican congress people and the republican-based radio talk host refuses to work with the pompous democrat congress people. It's such a mess. Ideologically I would have wanted to revere my congressmen and congresswomen for representing me to my nation. For them to take up the noble causes that would heal this country of its woes, and for them to do it only because it was what they went to Washington to do. Just being honest. Now it's all about power and money. So sad.

The Family Broke

(1981) – There is a phrase in this song that goes, *"though my heart burned and ached, I never showed it on my face."* It was from the essence of the emotional impact and psychology of that phrase that I wrote this whole piece. It's probably no secret that this song is about divorce; more specifically about my own father, Jack Baldwin and my own mother,

Eva Ruth Scarbrough, Kaiser, Baldwin and their parting, along with all the stark and subtle ramifications of what happens when a family loses its direction from the parental leadership, and the confusion that reigns after the love has become secondary or non-consequential, so as to say, according to which the rightness or wrongness of it all depends, at least in part, on something other than the (non-moral) goodness or badness of the consequences.

This has been come to be known as my **"first BIG HURT"** of which it took years for me to be at peace with, and because of Senior's unwillingness to embrace fatherhood with his step children, I was well into my twenties before I moved on.

It would seem though, that divorce reaps many more victims than just the couple. We, the children, had a lot to lose in that divorce; brothers and half-brothers and step brothers all being divided and divvied up like dumping a bag of penny candy out on the floor to be sure everybody gets their share.

From left to right and top to bottom:
Edward, 8, David, 9, John, 10, Jack, 11,
Chester, 4, Richard, 3, Raymond, 5

Nowadays, in many cases, when divorces happen, older children are sometimes given choices to choose which of the parents they would go with. This was not the case with my mother and father who seemed to dissolve their marriage too quickly after the mistakes had been made. My father, who came into this marriage with two boys, Jack and Ed, decided to take them and my brother Ray, strictly on the reason that Ray was a mini-me of my father and they both had red hair. My mother, who came into this marriage also with two boys, John and David, left with them, and took Richard, and myself. There's more to why Ray did not go with us, but that story is told in, 'Stepping Between The Ants - Book TWO: The Spring Ahead,' I believe.

And so, this wonderful family that had seven boys, split apart and the closeness that we all had at that one time, never happened again; some of which, like John and Jack who were really close and for seven years, did everything together, never saw or even spoke to each other again.

Ray is still close to brothers Jack and Ed, while Ritchie and I are still close to John and David along with Senior's children, Charlie and Mary (who came later), and I still have a strong bridge with my brother Ray, but I'm not close enough to Jack for him to ever accept me as his brother and Ed, well I think Ed has never really liked me; he's tolerated me and my stupid flippant remarks that I might have made back in the late '60s to gain acceptance from him and be the funny brother he never had, but it wasn't taken in the spirit it was given, and I set some kind of warped model in motion that I was never able to amend or escape from.

It would seem that some of the scars left from divorce will never heal. Moreover, I don't believe people with children would jump into that divorce syndrome so quickly if they only realized just how screwed up their children might end up and all because of a parent's inability to forgive, unwillingness to communicate through the problems or feed into their selfish needs.

Waiting

(1986) – There comes a time in the life of the abuser where the realization comes to him that she's gone and is probably not coming back to him, and if that person has a conscience, it has to hurt to know that he went too far and has no one to blame but himself. When I originally wrote this piece back in 1986 it had a good, slow, driving beat and melancholy message. I will say that when I prepared to record this song, my intentions were to follow that original concept, but somehow in the process of recording and engineering the mix-down, this song transformed into something entirely different.

The second song on this album is about how the family broke, and I followed that with this song because this looked at the separation or divorce process from the eyes of him who was the motivating force to have everyone leave and the reason in the end he was left to himself. At first, I started writing this, trying to bring it out from the perspective of Senior, but I found it hard to get into the mindset of someone I didn't really know, (nor ever tried to get close enough to know), so afterwards, I was left with trying to reflect a person that was probably wrong and had made some mistakes but had had some passion and desire to put it all back together again and try to work things out. I thought of myself sitting in an empty house staring at the walls analyzing my mistakes and wondering, just wondering if I could put anything back together again, my life, our life, could I ever get her to come back and do I deserve or can I ever be trusted again.

I Know

(1973) – Right after we got married, we moved into a nice little brick apartment in the northwest section of Portland. We stayed at this apartment for six months until it was more than obvious that we were, that is to say Diane was great with child. Afterwards we moved to the Chinese Castle where a new life awaited both of us. I was very happy there for quite some time and my creativity and a lot of songs grew from that time and place.

Not more than a week after Lori was born Diane became, let's just say, moody and I found myself dealing with a whole new person, a whole new personality, I found myself dealing with a girl that was now a mother. This new mother had some strange mood swings that were crazy and I was never sure when I would be dealing with this dilemma, and so I was not sure what to say or not to say and how to act, but because I still loved her, I adjusted and just tried to work with it.

This song is about that time and that era and that struggle that we went through in the beginning of our marriage.

Side Note:

Although I have sang this song many times to Diane, I don't know that she remembers the origins of it or the reason I wrote this song to begin with,... but I know.

There was a moment when in the Chinese Castle where Diane felt like she couldn't be the mother she needed to be and we were sitting around in the living room when she started crying. Okay, I have a hard time when the baby cries, but now I'm dealing with this emotional woman that didn't want to talk about it, only wanted me to listen. And as her best friend, there are decisions that must be made and consequences to my words and actions if not done right. As I said, she didn't want me to speak up, only listen, which I politely did until the baby, (Lori) woke up and was hungry, so Diane laid her in our bed, began nursing her and fell asleep. I then wrote the song and went to bed myself. Next morning when she woke, everything had changed. She wasn't sad anymore, she thanked me for being a good listener, and I got a song out of it. Good trade, I think.

Where Were You?

(1991) – During that creative era in 1991 I wrote so many songs that many of them just became documentations to fill books and become part of my ongoing database. Just prior to me recording this album I rediscovered this tune and worked it over to become the song that you hear now.

Side Note:

Although not related to the concept of "Where Were You," most of the occurrences in this song indeed did happen to me. I was threatened, not by the Bank but by our insurance company, I lived for years in trailer town, I had a problem with our septic system, of course, my 67 Chevy broke down, (electrical problem – a big block resister on the firewall, who knew?) and I had to walk to work, and although most of the stuff happened here and there, it was all right around the same time when I was either unemployed, trying to go to school or after I started working for the Washington State Parks and also going back and forth to the college.

I therefore incorporated all the dishevelment and hassle; that feeling of being helplessness overwhelmed as everything is falling apart, all seemingly at the same time, that and the knowledge that I will be on the front line to fix things because we had little to no money and it was my job. I must let you folks out there reading this know, not at first, but a bit later on when the kids were relatively bigger, there were a lot of fixing done collectively with and be Diane. She would help do the breaks and let me tell you, when it comes to working on cars, two bodies and four hands are much better than one and two. She also got good, well let's say, no, let's say good at working on appliances. Together we tackled a few top-loading washing machines and we worked on many different dryers, which basically only break down because of three things, the heating elements, the belt to drive the drum and the motor driving the belt. The timer on top went out once but that was a fluke. I have found that Diane has a good sense of how things work just by looking at the insides.

Another Side Note:

As mentioned before, I write a lot of material with other artists in mind and with this song I was thinking about Dolly Parton because I love her versatile, lyrical and pleasant-sounding voice and she seems to have an ability to convey to her listeners the, "dealing with disappointment" subject pretty well and bonus; she has a way of expressing a lot of sentiment and emotion that I would like to hear.

Yet Another Side Note:

From all the stuff I have had to tackle over the years, stuff I was never too good at,... cars are the worst. Nowadays where we don't have mechanics fixing cars anymore, we now have technicians because manufacturers have taken the process and totally complicated things by cramming all that other stuff in so the average Joe can't even change the water pump without taking the dang motor out.

But before, working on vehicles years ago was not that complicated and I would do all the work myself, and if I couldn't do it, I had my good friend Mike Wilmoth do it. In those days driving a clunker or POS meant you were going to have problems; it was always just a matter of when. Enter my 67 Chevy Nova. There wasn't much I  didn't know about that car, (didn't mean I could fix everything), but it was a simpler time. The Nova broke down on me all the time. And when the Chevy had problems, Diane would show up with the 'Green Pickle' van and 25 feet of chain and tow me back home,... and then I would have to figure out what was wrong and how to fix it. It broke down on my way to back to SPSCC at the same time I needed to take an accounting test. I got there 30 minutes late to a one-hour test and the professor, Nap (Napoleon) Lucchini told me I could not take a make up test,... he was strict and to the letter and I barely passed his class.

Another time, I was coming from SPSCC to go to the Washington State Parks Department when the car broke down by Tumwater on the two-lane southbound I5 freeway,... and it was morning rush hour,... and there was no shoulder,... That was an embarrassing moment as cars were backed up past the Olympia 101 exit and eventually a WS State Highway Patrolman had to push my off the freeway and to a gas station,... I could go on but why? You get the picture.

But the thing is, both Lori and Chet eagerly learned how to drive a stick shift, (three on the tree) with this 67 Chevy),... and although for Lori it was better than driving the big van,... but for Chet, driving the 67 Chevy was something special,... and try and imagine how cool it would be for you to drive something like the, (POS), 67 Chevy to school? I know I would have loved to be able to drive a cool classic like that when I was in high school,...

I Just Might Die Tonight

(1968) – This is one of my oldest songs to survive from my first days of songwriting. It documents my need to be a nonconformist and to stand up for what I believe is right. I can still remember that there was a study hall where the students were brought into a gymnasium and after witting in the risers, were told to do their homework. I found this ineffectual because all my classes that needed homework were held after this work study time. So with my black Bic pen and my spiral notebook, I started writing poems, (that, sometime in the future might be converted to be lyrics).

I entered this poem, (for poem it was back then), into a contest at the Pemberton Township High School Talent Search, right after Thanksgiving, thinking it was hot stuff and hoping for that time that I could recite it to the whole student body in the auditorium. I practiced reciting it again and again, sometimes in front of a mirror to make sure I had the right look. I never found out if I'd won or was even a consideration in the contest, because during Christmas vacation my mother, along with Ritchie and I, flew to Portland Oregon under the auspices that we were just visiting,... mostly to pay our last respects to my revered Grandpa Scarbrough, who had recently passed away, and afterwards, I never returned back to New Jersey,... but instead Richie and I ended up on the farm with my dad and I finished out my Senior year at North Marian High School in Donald Oregon. But that whole thing, that episode, is indeed another story for another time.

Come And Share It With Me

(1971) – Even back in 1971 I was ecologically and environmentally concerned and aware of my surroundings, proved by this strange little song that chronicles problems with pollution, forest management, conservation, greed and deprivation of third-world countries as well as the overall masses, inflation, problematic denial and governmental hypocrisy. Sarcastically, as I sing this song, I'm asking you to not only listen to what I sing about, I'm asking you to partake of the problems and share those problems with me, or more precisely, that we share the problems together, and that we can make a change, in spite of the apathy of non-believers, in spite of the lacking spirit or something that is known to have problems; we all stand partially responsible for many of the problems of the world.

Side Note:

In July of 1974 I made arrangements and eventually went over to KBOO; a non-profit, listener-funded FM Community radio station broadcasting from Portland, Oregon. I brought with me my 1963 Fender King acoustic guitar along with a sorted collection of harmonicas, (I borrowed Louie's A harmonica (which I had recently given him), because mine was dead,... and towards the end of the fifth song, *"The Mud Puddle"* if you listen closely, I can be heard thanking Louie for the loan). I was rather nervous, not having played at a radio station before,...

and the thought that hundreds if not maybe even thousands of people would get the chance to listen to Lord Baldwin was awesome,... but maybe not in the good sense you might think,... I was worried that I might screw up here and there causing people to turn me off and worse, remember it was Lord Baldwin that was, *'Just Not Good Enough'*,...

Me playing on KBOO Radio station in Portland – July of 1974

I believe it was in the early afternoon when I finally got set up to play. To be sure, there was an assumption on my part, maybe from an agreement over the phone, but I think I was told that I would only be doing a couple of songs, and so I still over prepared and came in, planning to do a 15-minute set,...

Little did I know that they would want me to do three times that,... but, like the good Boy Scouter I was, I came prepared with all my paperwork in a folder,... and instead of doing three to five songs, I ended up doing 18 songs; which, because of adrenalin in my system, sped up every song and eventually only took me about 45 minutes to sing all my songs.

This song, *"Come And Share It With Me"* was the 14th of the songs and came past the halfway point in my performance. If nothing else, the performance was well received by the disc jockeys and other staff listening,... One guy came over to me as I was putting my gear away and said that he thought I was like, another **Jim Croce**.

I Was Here A Long Time Ago

(1991) – Pre-being preexistence, beforelife, or premortal existence is a concept and part of the foundation of the beliefs within the LDS church and is the belief that each individual human soul existed before mortal conception, and at some point before birth enters or is placed into the body. Concepts of pre-existence can encompass either the belief that the soul came into existence at some time prior to conception or the belief that the soul is eternal. Alternative positions are traducianism; a doctrine about the origin of the soul or synonymously, spirit, holding that this immaterial aspect is transmitted through natural generation along with the body, the material aspect of human beings, and creationism; holding that the origin of the soul cannot be by spiritual generation from the souls of parents because human souls, being essentially and integrally simple and indivisible, can give forth no spiritual germs or reproductive elements, which both hold that the individual human soul does not come into existence until conception. It is to be distinguished from preformation, which is about physical existence and applies to all living things. Ancient Greek thought, and Islam affirms pre-existence, but is generally denied in most other Christianity beliefs.

The idea in this song is that before I was born, I was an intelligence in the spirit world waiting for my opportunity to partake of the process of being born and placed into a family.

This song continues on to document the witnessing or at least the watching of the creation of the earth, the coming of man and his posterity, and the excitement and thrill of the possibility of my own birth to happen.

The last verse deals with the loss of memory after birth but hints of remembering something or maybe a confirmation in my heart that something special was happening before I got here. Latter-day Saints refer to forgetting these memories as a veil, and they often refer to the premortal life as "the first estate." The veil of forgetfulness of the first estate apparently will not be suddenly, automatically, and totally removed at the time of our temporal death. This veil, a condition of our entire second estate, is associated with and is part of our time of mortal trial, testing, proving, and overcoming by faith—and thus will continue in some key respects into the spirit world.

Where Are You Now?

(1989) – I didn't write much in 1989; I was just holding onto whatever I could, and because I knew JW Electronics was dying, and although I was cool and calm on the outside, inside I was nervously worried about the future of the Baldwin family,… There would be times where I would pray for divine intervention and deliverance from my adverse circumstances but it was not my time for that to happen,… Instead, I was blessed with everything we needed at the time,… and although my inner depression issues seemed to overshadow any hope of inspiration for any new songwriting, this song materialized,… and it is therefore kind of special, in spite of the fact that it is kind of a downer in and of itself,.., but still, this song managed to creep out, even during this relatively depressing time.

Side Note:

This song is about a relationship that I had; a relationship that slowly dissolved, even as I tried to keep it going with continued interactions and communications. I had met Linda Marie in New Jersey at the Pemberton Township High School (in choir class), and when we found that we lived six blocks away from each other in Browns Mills, we started hanging out with each other,… and we became good friends,…

Linda Marie lived with her mother in a small house adjacent to some woods that we would explore from time to time. Linda Marie was a brain;… she was on the honor roll, excelling in everything, science, math, music, (she played piano very well, played an oboe in orchestra and pounded out a glockenspiel for marching band),... and she was crazy disciplined when it came to doing her homework,... but she was alone all the time,... her mother was almost always gone, usually to a boyfriend's house, who was one of the teachers at Pemberton Township,... Linda Marie's mother and boyfriend were both big on drinking beer and chain-smoking cigarettes,... and I remember being amazed and wondered how these two adults could easily polish off a 24-bottle case of beer when, if I drank just one beer, I was feeling drunk, (never did like the taste of beer anyway),... but I shouldn't have been too surprised knowing that Senior could tackle the most part of a gallon of wine.

Anyway, Linda Marie could be found at my place more than me at her place because she especially liked my

ten-year-old sister Mary,... and anyway, being alone all the time at her house, all she had to look forward to was getting her homework done so she could reward herself with a TV dinner.

Long story short; Linda Marie moved to Reno Nevada summer of 1968 because her mother's boyfriend, who was a teacher, got a job with one of the schools there, and I moved from New Jersey to the Oregon at the beginning of 1969, and after graduating from North Marion High School, (Donald Oregon), I hitchhiked to Reno.

At first, it seemed like everything was great. After working in a few smaller casino restaurants, I got a good job, working for Harrah's as a Food Service Manager and I was making a decent salary. Moreover, even though my hours were from 3:00 AM to 11:00 AM, (which included a half-hour break for lunch and two 15-minute breaks), which didn't give me an ability for a lot of quality time in a relationship, I felt we were making it work.

It was mid-summer when I started to feel a rough, cooler breeze in our relationship; the closeness and warmth factor seemed to be strained. At first, I felt that it was an uncertainty coming from Linda Marie, but it would be weeks before I realized that it was her mother that had been subtly turning our relationship off. And her mother didn't want her daughter Linda Marie, that had scored so high on her SAT, to lose focus on her college educational goals, especially after receiving scholarships, and after already having been excepted to some prestigious schools, including the University of Nevada, which was right there in Reno.

Linda Marie and I had had some different plans, but nothing that didn't include her college education,... but I came to find out that her mother's big plans and dreams for her scholastic daughter eventually did not include the likes of a dead beat like me,...

I kind of felt like there was something going on when I had come over to their apartment on July 20, 1969 to watch the moon landing. She was there, kind of excited to see me; her mother and her mother's boy-friend; not so much. As Commander Neil Armstrong and lunar module pilot Buzz Aldrin landed the Apollo Lunar Module, Eagle,... there was a lot of excitement in the air and hearing me happily conversing with her daughter, her mother asked Linda Marie about Bob,... Linda Marie looked embarrassed as she replied that she hadn't seen Bob in days and then quickly turned to me to explain that Bob was one of the college recruiters from the University of Nevada,... and that he had come to the apartment to talk to Linda Marie about her academic plans to go there,...

The kicker was that he had come back a couple of times, mostly for a social visit and she assured me that there wasn't anything between them,... but the damage; the lost trust,... it was already done, and as I looked over at her mother, seeing a sly, smarmy Mrs. Robinson's smile as she looked away, I knew how she felt about me and that I was indeed, in trouble.

Close to the end of summer, during the big push to go through the admissions processes to go to college,... I was suddenly and deliberately met with a renewed, strong indifference from her mother who, when I went to their house see Linda Marie, had no problem lying to me and telling me that Linda Marie wasn't home at that time; anything to just to get rid of me or put me off for some other time later,... meanwhile, I had no idea if Linda Marie had found another boyfriend in the mix; (maybe Bob),... maybe someone else,... but I continued waiting for the opportunity to try to put our relationship back together again,... but by now, I couldn't get past the gatekeeper with my visits or even phone calls. After a while I could see that it was all in vain because Linda Marie didn't seem to have any intention of trying to reconstruct our relationship.

The last time I saw Linda Marie was when I went over to her apartment and was greeted by her mother, who told me that Linda Marie wasn't home,... but I looked past her mother and saw Linda Marie with her back to me in the kitchen animatedly talking to someone on the telephone.

In the end, I left Reno with slight disenchantment and hitchhiked back to Oregon,... and for a while, in a melancholy way, I would reflect back on that, long ago and far away time, where there was that someone that I was close to, that I was ready to spend my life with; that someone that broke my heart and eventually let me go. And for a while I did wonder, where is she now?

64

- 26 - Work - 1993 -

65

NOTES ABOUT THE COVERS

Notes On The New Cover:

During the great depression there was a migration to get to somewhere where work could be found. Apparently, these folks had to endure a lot of hardship in their journeys. I just loved the determination on the father's face that seemed to say, "I'm doing this." And the indominable spirit he must have had to lead his family to the promised land. (and notice they brought their dog)

Notes On The Original Covers:

I have a fear of heights and so what these men were doing in 1926, sitting on a steel girder hundreds of feet in the air eating their lunch,... Nothing less than amazing to me,... Notice wings with lettering on this back cover in my attempt to make the back cover fit in plastic cd sleeves. In Browns

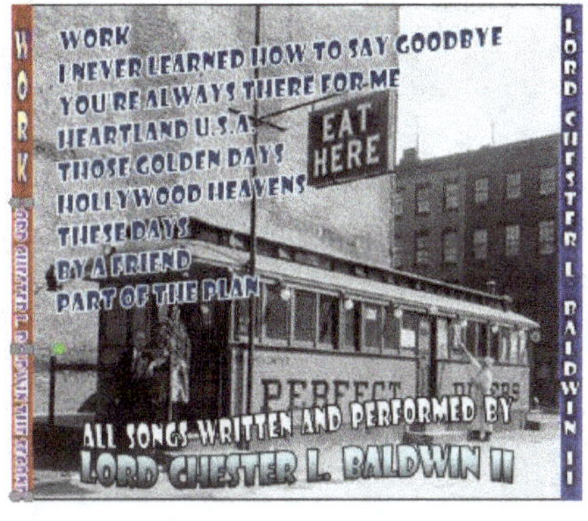

Mills New Jersey there used to be one of these diners where I would go and have a cup of tea.

66

WORK

Work
I Never Learned How To Say Goodbye
Always There For Me
Heartland U.S.A.
Those Golden Days
Hollywood Heavens
(Instrumental)
These Days
By A Friend
Part Of The Plan

67

Work

Puts his steel-toed boots on his feet;
Grabs his lunch box and hardhat off the seat.
Clips his nail belt on and puts his hammer away,
heads out on the project for another long day
of work; work.
Work; work.

Commission or not, sales got to be made;
obligations and bills need to be paid.
Every word is weighed and he knows what to say,
as he grabs another line for another long day
of work; work.
Work; work.

The day drags on; the time draws near;
in his anger for all the reasons he's here.
He works at the endless shift as his life fades away,
his dreams repressed; he braces for another long day
of work; work.
Work; work.

Repetition is all the belt-chain brings.
Day in, day out as he's doing the same thing.
He wants to use his head;
think and plan out the future way,
but instead is just resigned to another long day
of work; work.
Work; work.

Handling the remains; every call out of town.
Pick them up, fix them right; go lay them down.
And the long day turns to night
and the nighttime starts to fade
to the never-ending saga of another long day
of work; work.
Work; work.

68

I Never Learned How To Say Goodbye

As I was growing up, all my feelings of true love
were confused by all I went through in my home.
My mother loved a man that I could hardly stand
step-father to a son he'd never know.
Don't know what went on behind closed doors and closed minds
I only saw them vaguely happy now and then.
He'd treat her rough and bad and she'd leave with the kids in hand,
but she'd always seem to go back there again.

Seems she never learned how to say goodbye to her hard times.
She just kept looking for the change that would turn
everything around.
There was something wrong
but she just couldn't see all the dark signs
of a good love turned bad and a last dream falling down.

Some people never learn from the past and its rough turns.
When to hold on tight or when to let things go.

I thought I'd change the world when I met that special girl,
but I couldn't see the undercurrent's flow.
Although our love was strong
something somewhere just went wrong,
that I couldn't piece together along the way.
I see her troubled ways and I hope to see them change,
and it's that hope that carries me from day to day.

Seems I've never learned how to say goodbye to my hard times.
I just kept looking for the change that would turn
everything around.
There was something wrong,
but I just wouldn't see all the dark signs
of a good love turned bad and a last dream falling down.

Seems we never learn how to say goodbye to our hard times.
We just keep looking for the change that will turn
everything around.
Though there's something wrong,
we just won't see all the dark signs
of a good love turned bad and a last dream falling down;
of a good love turned bad and a last dream falling down.

69

You're Always There For Me

In my desperate hour of need,
so unsure and afraid,
you were there for me,
behind me all the way.
When it seemed like no one cared,
I was so lost and alone,
but you were always there
to help and bring me home,
and lift my spirit free;
you're always there for me.
Seems I only come around
when my world falls apart;
in the lost and found,
contrite spirit and broken heart.
You always take me in,
a lost and lonely lamb,
to see the good within
loving me for who I am.
I turn around and see
you're always there for me.

70

Heartland U.S.A.

There was a time ago; a not so distant place,
before the farms were auctioned off and the kids all moved away.
Off the side; a gravel road; a shaded house and lawn,
where things were like that farmhouse; simple, good and strong.
Families all had purpose then; a cause for everyone.
Early to bed, early to rise, with so much to be done.
A time to work, a time to rest, a time to share the way.
A time to love and be loved, in heartland U.S.A.

Heartland U.S.A.; Heartland U.S.A.

Neighbors trusting neighbors, had no fool to harbor greed.
A good dog on the porch at night was all we'd ever need.
Hand to hand, eye to eye, integrity carried through,
and it was all right back then to be honest, chaste and true.
Values seemed so basic; we would pick up where we fall.
Good living was its own reward; God blessed us, one and all.
Life was not perfect, but a far cry from today,
the seeds of thought to harvest from Heartland U.S.A.

Heartland U.S.A.; Heartland U.S.A.

In the land of the brave and the home of the free,
there's a whisper of sorrow in the wind through the trees.

Times and values changing; the world seems to grow small,
and we become a part of everything around us all.
Farmers, all but ruined; with no recourse but to sell,
are victims of this age, they foresaw as it fell.
The progress must move forward as we cadence into place,
can't we see the damage and the loss we'll have to face.
We've boxed up our heritage and sold it all away;
all we saved were the photographs of Heartland U.S.A.

Heartland U.S.A.; Heartland U.S.A.

Though we priced it high, with a profit of bones,
in the end we deprived the children of their own.
Their Heartland U.S.A.,
Heartland U.S.A.

71

Those Golden Days

All those golden days, they keep on coming,
all those days, they just keep on running.
And me; I'm just getting closer to old.

That old man time doesn't care how it feels,
he is laughing at us while we're under his wheels.
Telling us, so we know there's no deals to be made.

And I don't know where it went, like a ghost it went past.
Can't see how it all got spent,
like a shadow it just didn't last.

Seems like only yesterday, I had so much time to play,
but now I'm rolling down this hill,
and I Got no breaks to stand still.

all those golden days, they just keep on coming,
all those days, they just keep me running,
And me, I'm just getting closer to old.

All those silver words appear untarnished,
diamond photographs, all flower garnished
to keep the past well polished yet,

I still don't know where it went, like a ghost it went past.
I can't see how it all got spent,
like a shadow it just didn't last.

Seems like only yesterday, I had so much time to play,
but now I'm rolling down this hill,
and I Got no breaks to stand still.

And those golden days, they just keep on coming,
all those days, they just keep on running.
And me, I'm just getting closer to old.

72

These Days

Everywhere I look around, I see my good friends going down.
Letting go of things they please,
their house, their wife and families.

Why even try to work things out or put up with opposing doubt,
when all you need to change the rent
is a divorce and a settlement.

These days are getting harder to have devotion to one and the same,
while everyone is running out; playing the cheating game.

All my old friends downtown, are quite unsettled from falling out.
Loss of benefits, pension free,
loss of reason for loyalty.

Work the years, retire old, to find there's nothing saved at all.
They worked the system as a friend,
to get the shaft;
a premature end.

These days are getting harder to be committed to the boss,
while everyone is running out of the system and the laws.

Everyday between the wedge I get closer to the cutting edge.
Money's tight; the prices high;
consumers fight; people lie.

In the middle of the economy dive trying hard to stay alive.
Friends give in to the American dream,
lose their home and dignity.

These days are getting harder to avoid the back-street lines,
while everyone is running out of hope for better times.

Can't help but fear the worst is now, and feel a hopelessness
around.
Christians fighting for some past
where love is all that should be cast.

Chasing fool's gold with no goals, as many sell their lives and souls.
Friends, once strong, now walk the streets
and throw up their hands in sad defeat.

These days are getting harder to have faith in all your dreams,
while everyone is running out of everything you believe.

73

By a Friend

People spend their lives in search
for that heart of special worth.
Some reach in vain until the end,
when all they wanted was love by a friend.

People take time; making sure relationships for good endure.
Emotions fly to make amends
to touch the fragile heart of a friend.

We have the need that draws us near,
and yet we hesitate with fear.
The shy retreats; unsure descends,
relating between walls of a friend.

Living with all the bright machines, of comforts and securities,
yet all I own, I'd gladly lend,
and forsake for the love of a friend.

Like the child that stands up tall,
that looks for good and trusts in all,

with arms outstretched for love extends
the need, the hope, the passion to be friends.

The changing times and progress new with no time given to pursue;
a the precious gift to share and send
is love and trust to always be a friend.

74

Part Of The Plan

The last days are upon us now my friend.
I feel sorry for he who knows and yet pretends.
Afraid to be committed, he'll run down all he could believe.
Yet, knowing deep inside where he should be,
but that won't be me.

For a time, I've felt the changes of these days.
I've been wrestling with my past to change my ways.
To be prepared for callings, my life will carry through.
If you could only sense the things I do, you'd plot out yours too.

It's all part of the plan, living life as good and best we can.
Lengthening our stride to stretch our span.
Trying to become a perfect man.
never worry about rewards that we could spend,
just living the laws and enduring to the end.

My family is not perfect, but we hope to be;
we are try to work together in harmony.
Putting out the selfish thoughts that could isolate our home,

from the love and charity, we need to own, to carry on.

It's all part of the plan, living life as good and best we can.
Lengthening our stride to stretch our span.
Trying to become a perfect man.
Never worry about rewards that we could spend,
just living the laws and enduring to the end.

and the last days are upon us now my friend;
there's so much we need to do before the end.
Above all, we need to reach out to our brothers and their needs.
To love all, unconditionally; then we might all see,

That it's all part of the plan, living life as good and best we can.
Lengthening our stride to stretch our span.
Trying to become a perfect man;
never worry about rewards that we could spend,
just living the laws and enduring to the end.

75

MEMOIRS & NOTES - 26 - 'WORK'

Work

(1993) – In 1993 I recorded 10 albums, using a lot of material I had already written years earlier, combined with newer songs that were writing around that time.

The album, "Work," was the last of these 10 albums and contained only one new song, this one, "Work," all the rest were written prior to 1993.

Although I didn't get to know him till I was a senior in high

school, my dad was the epitome of the loyal, dedicated working man. He drove a delivery truck for Meier & Franks Department store in the Portland Oregon area.

During the Regan administration a conglomerate purchased Meier & Franks and using Reganomics, got rid of the package delivery services and eventually, after shifting him for a couple months to furniture delivery, they forced my dad into early retirement.

My original idea for this song was to take a cameo, so to speak, of all the occupations that I had worked, and kind of weave them into little snippets of my life. Unfortunately, due to my diverse employment past, there were far too many verses for me to represent myself throughout my working life, but I managed to grab much of my working past to encapsulate the essence into this song.

I started with my days in construction when I was working as a construction laborer in Portland Oregon. Next, I chose my occupation in phone sales as a telecommunicator at JW Electronics, where I worked in parts and product sales. Next, I dealt with my frustration and unhappiness working in many of the menial jobs and occupations along the way, like when I worked at Georgia-Pacific as a laborer and cardboard stacker (they called me a Pilot; that is to say, pick it up off the green belt and *pile it* here and then, *pile it* there), as a Busboy at the Hilton in Portland, and a Waiter in upstate NY in the Catskills, (the Concord Hotel, the Pines, Shenks and the Raleigh), a Dishwasher at Harrah's in Reno, (where I worked quickly up to Food Manager), a Draftsman at Burns and Row International Construction Inc., and there were various landscaping jobs, a Short Order Cook, a Soda Jerk, all in Kiamesha Lakes in Upstate NY, and a sundry of others. The last verse dealt with some of my feelings and experiences as a funeral director and embalmer, and perhaps most of all some of my disappointments with all my lost time working that long, never-ending shift and trudging through the never-ending work day (or night).

It is good to note that there was something gained from every job I worked. Sometimes I was able to build upon the new job with skills learned prior, like at Harrah's or the at the funeral home. Also, I was in charge of setting markers and such in the cemetery and I had developed good skills doing flatwork. I even redid other poorly done markers or fixed broken markers.

Work is an important part of everyone's life whether they gained skills from them or learned just what jobs were not good and what to stay away from, and the many faceted perspectives of these different occupations came experiences that have been good for me, and experiences that I carried with me to other occupations and draw on to this day.

Side Note:

It was February something in 1958, David and I were on our way back from the Braumart theater with me precariously perched on the front handlebars of David's bike heading up North Stephenson Avenue.

On the corner, just before turning down Margaret Street was an A&W root beer stand and in the window was a sign that read, "Help Wanted." David purposely hit a curb divider causing me to fall forward, landing on all fours. David smiled as he walked towards the door but seeing me following him, he turned and said, "You wait here and protect the bike." David walked inside and I could see him through the windows talking to a tall thin older man. David sort of smiled, shaking his head before he suddenly turned around and I could see him pointing to me. Seeing that I was looking at them, David motioned for me to come in there with him. I pointed to the bike of which David got an annoyed look on his face before waving again for me to join him. As I was coming in I could hear David say, "This is the guy you need to work here." Looking confused, I stopped moving forward. "Skipper," David said motioning for me to come closer, "this man here wants to give you a job."

"I never said that I,.." The man interrupted, "I'm looking for some-one older."

David laughed and said, "Skipper here can do the job alright, and he lives just three blocks down the street."

The man looked me over a second time and said, "Well, maybe,..."

"Hey, hey," David said dismissively, "Looks like you got yourself a job."

"I never said,..." the man began. "But I guess we can try you out and see how you do." He turned to me and said, "You ready to go to work?"

With confusion I looked at David who smiled triumphantly and said, "I'll see you later. Don't forget to bring me my root beer when you're done." And with that said, David walked outside, got on his bike and left me there.

It was my job to go out into the parking lot and pick up all the gar-bage and debris that had been left on the lot, including cigarette butts, wrappers, bags of unfinished food and the recently invented and now infamous, aluminum ketchup packets that were everywhere, ground into the asphalt by cars that purposely ran over them to have the ketchup blast out of the packets. And as you can see from the picture, the parking lot was ginormous, especially to an eight-year-old. Still, I was wondering why David didn't want the job, except for the packets, it really wasn't that hard and I was done in about two hours.

When I went inside and let my new boss know I was done, he poured a draft of root beer in an official A&W mug and placed it on the counter. He grabbed a take-out container and filled it with root beer and set it next to the draft. "This one," the man said, pointing to the draft, "is for you." As I took a sip, he pointed to the take-out cup and said, "This is for your brother,... this time only." He looked out at the parking lot and said, "Next Saturday morning and Sunday."

As I was finishing the root beer the man opened up the cash register and pulled out a quarter and handed it to me. "Thanks." I said, thinking I'd just got the best job ever. "Oh," the man said smiling, "you can keep the glass mug too."

When I got home, I handed David his root beer and then as I showed him, mother and Richie the glass mug I asked, "David, why didn't you take the job?"

"A quarter?" David quizzed. "And you were there working for two hours in the freezing cold? For a root beer and a quarter? No thanks, that's chump change."

"Well, I wouldn't mind working there." Richie said jealously, eyeing the quarter in my hand, "It's not fair Skipper gets a job and I,..."

"Richie, you're seven." Mother replied. "I'm not sure I want Skipper there either."

That next Saturday I was there working when Richie sheepishly creeped up and stood there watching me work.

"Go home." I commanded as I looked over at him angrily. "You want me to lose my job?"

Before Richie could answer, the boss man stepped out to where we were and seeing Richie, the boss man said, "This your brother?" As I nodded, he said, "I don't usually have enough work for two, but last night we got hammered. He turned to Richie and said, "You wanna help your brother?"

The smile on Richie's face was affirmation enough and when we were done we each got a root beer float and a quarter, and,.. he let us keep the mugs again.

I continued to work there (off and on with Richie), until we finally left for the last time in 1963. By then we had a cupboard full of A&W mugs, which, sadly, stayed there in Michigan because we were running away yet again from Senior and could only take essentials.

I Never Learned How To Say Goodbye

(1986) – There are a lot of people out there that live in relationships that are strained and they live with it, hoping things might be different sometime later. My mother professed to be a big fan of my music and every time I created a new album or to be precise two albums, she always got a copy of my work. When I finished doing this song, I had second thoughts about sending this album to my mother, due to the fact that this song could be touching on a subject that could be too sensitive. And I did not want any ill feelings or to create an alienation between her and I. But, as it turned out, there was really nothing to worry about, because she understood where I was coming from and where the lyrics to this song were going.

This tune came to me about the fall of 1986 after listening to the news and hearing about studies that claimed that most children had a tendency of following in the footsteps of their parent's habits and mannerisms, even when their parent's examples were far from

Mother – June of 1996

exemplary or moreover, damaging, cruel or corrupt. I tinkered around with some phrases in words and banged around my guitar until something clicked. I then took this song within a prospective of me watching and evaluating my mother from how she dealt with her failed relationships only to disingenuously or unknowingly repeatedly mirror her ways. I then put myself in the same mold with my own debouched relationships. This was a bit of a stretch considering the fact that, because I had such a difficult childhood, due to our life and times with Senior, and because I never wanted to be anything like him, my ideal relationship was foundational on a very strong trust and monogamous relationship. Nonetheless, the phrase, (or hook), "I never learned how to say goodbye to my hard times," was just too good to let go.

Side Note:

in August of 1996 my mother became gravely ill from an infection after she had had chemotherapy and all of us brothers (and sister Mary), rallied to her bedside in a hospital in Miami. Her husband, Ron Davis, who had been married to her now for about 25 years, went totally weird on us. He was as nice as pie to all of us to our face collectively, but he started drinking, and when drunk, became disingenuously duplicitous, crafty and generally insincere. It was like when he got drunk, he felt it was okay for him to take off the mask that he had to wear when sober, and the more he drank, the more he reminded me of Senior. He would argue for the sake of being contrary, often losing perspective of why he was arguing. At first, I tried to understand him, going through a grieving period himself for him to soon lose my mother, but in truth, he lacked the sense of sincerity or true love for my mother, even at this moment; her last moments here on earth.

It was my hope to retrieve all of my material that she had collected over the past ten years, but I felt it would be wrong to be rummaging through possessions without his permission. Moreover, mother had a Last Will & Testament of her own, that documented her wishes for the estate division and categorized those other things as well, with instructions on how she wanted her things, (money and personal possessions), administered and distributed.

Unfortunately, this "Will" mysteriously disappeared a few days before mother passed away, never to resurface again. And so, after a promise from Ron that everything; her stuff and all of her children's, would be gone through, separated, and passed out to those individuals, two weeks after mother passed away, Ron took everything in the household, all of her possessions as well as some of ours, sold everything for what he could get, and the rest went to the Goodwill. He then moved quietly and quickly away after he emptied the bank account and sold the house.

You're Always There For Me

(1991) – It is good to have someone that believes in you. It's also kind of neat to be able to write lyrics for a song saying one thing, but meaning another, or meaning both at the same time. It was my hope that someone later on might come to me and express their understanding, one way or the other or whatever, about this song. That never happened, maybe because nobody listened intently to the word of this song. But I cleverly jotted down the words to this song, using a parallel between a relationship with Jesus Christ and a relationship with a particular love and or good friend.

Side Note:

Working for the State was a dream come true for me. Never before did I get benefits. Never before did I have health care benefits so robust and encompassing as I was now getting. Never before did I have a payroll retirement plan, and never before did I make such money. The highest salary I had ever made before was $6.90 an hour. And now, even though I was still in school and had not gotten my degree yet, I was making more or less, $12.00 an hour. And even though we, (my family and I) were eligible for food stamps and even welfare to a small degree, Diane came to me and asked if we could try to do without them and just use my paycheck. I will not lie. With nine children, bills still coming in and after going through so many hard times I had issues like still-being-poor anxieties and I had strong food insecurities worrying about the kids and Diane and I, but in the end, we prayed about it and even though I did not get any strong inclinations one way or the other, we believed that if we paid our tithing the Lord would make sure we would have all we needed. And so, we dropped all assistance and never looked back.

Another Side Note:

After I got to know what it was that the job entailed at the Parks Dept. I happily excelled with everything I did; (everything except learning D-Base III to the extent that I needed, and in the end of my trial period would be my undoing and the supposed cause for me to have to move on).

But back to then, troubleshooting the network connectivity problems or understanding the software on the 386 computers at everyone's desks, I began making new friends every day. And reflecting on my past, I had never really had any female friends that I worked with. Don't get me wrong, I was and am happily married and I knew about the temptations that lurked in the shadows of the cubicles at the workplace, but I was right up front with everyone and did not allow any misunderstanding to give anybody the wrong idea. And all these new friends, men and women, became endeared with me when I brought things in from home; like pies made with cherries from my yard, cookies and coffee cakes, but the best, most revered thing for me to bring and share at work was Diane's bread. Iy was perfect. A lot of the women working there would have loved to eat the donuts others would bring in but there was always the self-incrimination to eating something that would cause them to put on weight. But bread, and especially Diane's bread was not a threat. Her bread is like eating a donut without the extra sugar outside. And they would ask me if I was going to bring more bread and when. It was good times.

Heartland USA

(1990) – Written in January of 1990, I was inspired to write the lyrics to this song after watching the news and seeing that a lot of our farmland in the Midwest was being sold off for tract housing. This news article went on in detail about the farmer's plight and lack of support from the state and federal government.

That same evening on the 6:00 news was an article talking about a growing trend in America where family values were deteriorating at an alarming rate. It also talked about the deterioration of the family unit itself and how this trend would affect our future,... and I worried for farmers like my dad who had a large garden to the right of Grandma Wicks place and who raised his own beef and pork and chickens and sheep,...

Moved by both of these news stories, I sat up late that night and wrote the lyrics. The next day, during my lunch hour at JW Electronics, I typed out the words, worked them around a bit and then brought the lyrics home for

My Dad's Farm in Aurora Ore. – circa 1990

musical interpretation. The only thing I had to work with, that I liked of the lyrics, was this, "Heartland USA." The rest vacillated between two different tones. This may sound funny or even kind of dumb, but after going back and forth with both of these tunes, I took the best part of both of them, combined chord progressions here and movements there and ultimately it worked out great.

Side Note:

by the time I typed out this poem at JW Electronics, the company was going down quickly. We were now counting down the weeks till the place would be closed. Sue, Jack Week's oldest daughter and sister to Diane, was now there at the store almost all the time. She was valuable to the place because she knew a little about everything in the store; was well versed with the inventory and assisted in accounting with her mother Mickey, and her other sister Kathy who was responsible for the books and did all the accounts receivable and accounts payable.

Another Side Note:

Onw day Jack Sr. was walking through the store followed by a parade of others,... Sue, Ron, (Kathy's husband) and Jackson, Diane's oldest brother,... all of which were trailing behind Jack Sr., making whatever activity Jack Sr. wanted to occur, or providing whatever answers needed to finalize things,... and making note of whatever action needed come to pass,... these three would cheerfully make things happen, and with kindnesses they would help Jack Sr. to get through this harrowing time of him losing almost everything and always with as much dignity and love as could possibly be given. I was the son-in-law or the brother-in-law or the guy working in the warehouse but at that time and during those trials, I was indeed family.

Golden Days

(1972) – This piano piece (and one other), marked a change in the style and direction of my musical capabilities with the piano. Written in 1972, during a small period of time while I was unemployed, this was one of the first pieces that I did not use a three/four (3/4) time, but instead shifted to a 4-4 time. This meant my left hand was going to have to work a little harder and it meant that I was going to have to think in different terms. Different terms of music, to meet the lyrics that would be presenting to the song itself. It was a challenge that I rose up to willingly but not without a lot of extra practice. The song itself is about a person whose time has quickly passed by and he is left looking back at little moments in his life, and realizes that he is now in his golden days. Kind of a funny thing to write about for a twenty-two-year-old, but it seemed right at the time. When I sang a song for the first time to my father and his wife Inez, both were unimpressed and unmoved. I thought at least my dad would appreciate the fact that I had practiced a lot. But I played it a lot because I had to get this 4-4 thing down,... and so it went, but this piece opened up a whole world of new musical possibilities.

Hollywood Heavens

(**Instrumental**) (1972) – I was at my dad's farm one Saturday afternoon and saw a news clip about how MGM was selling off a lot of props, memorabilia, costumes and end products like furniture, off the lot. Now you folks know my favorite movie is, "the Wizard of OZ," and then on the news show, there it was; the Ruby Slippers. And they were going to auction them off. My thoughts went out to the graveyard of stuff, like the ending of "Citizen Kane" and I thought of the place where Hollywood goes after the sun goes down.

To be sure, this was always supposed to have words. And in my head, connecting with the emotional music, words have come out. But I never felt like the words ever reached the passion or warm feeling that I have in that music. And so, this instrumental tune is the results.

Side Note:

at that time, in 1972, Louie's sister Laurie was dating a guy named, Gary Thompson, who had a pseudonym, Bill Scream. Bill was plugged into and doing a lot of commercials around Portland and Seattle, and he owned his own mobile recording studio, as well as a small recording studio in his basement. One day he asked me if I'd like to record some of my stuff and invited me to come to his home on a Sunday morning. We talked a lot about my material and just what we should do, but in the interim, we recorded *"Those Golden Days"* as well as, this tune, *"Hollywood Heavens,"* to gain a grasp of my voice range, and generally just to test the recording levels of the microphones to the machines. He was curiously impressed by the fact that I could play piano or guitar and sing at the same time because he could not. In fact, he told me that without a 4 or 8 track recording system, he would be lost, because he always recorded his music and then his voice over it. Just after we played around with and recorded *"Those Golden Days"* and *"Hollywood Heavens,"* and were ready to actually seriously record, Bill Scream got a call from someone that needed him and his portable recording studio right away. So he apologized and said that we would do it up right at another date. That other date never happened, but I think somewhere in my reel-to-reel archives I still have that practice session taped.

These Days

(1980) – Let me see if I can set this up so that you can understand where this song came from. Perhaps prophetically, one of the verses talks about the downsizing of America, which includes the insensitive posturing of letting go of their valuable, time-honored employees, which in fact became a growing trend during the Reagan administration in the '80s. The four pillars of Reagan's economic policy were, 1. to reduce the growth of government spending, 2. reduce the federal income tax and capital gains tax, 3. reduce government regulation, and, 4. tighten the money supply in order to reduce inflation,... but the end results was the disparaging widening income gap; an environment of greed, and the national debt tripling in eight years,... which ultimately reversed the post-World War II trend of a shrinking national debt as percentage of GDP,...

Also, under Reaganomics, the Social Security Amendments laid the foundation for more than 30-years of federal government's embezzlement of the Social Security money in order to use the money to pay for wars, tax cuts and other government programs.

And, the ultrarich had their taxes cut sharply — by about half. A millionaire who was then paying $700,000 on taxes in the 1970s saw their taxes cut to $350,000 in the 1980s.

One of the verses of the song refers to the attitude and feelings of frustration that we as Americans had as our fellow Americans were being held hostage in Iraq. The Iran Hostage Crisis was a diplomatic standoff between the United States and Iran. Fifty-two American diplomats and citizens

The Iran Hostage Crisis

were held hostage for 444 days from November 4, 1979, to January 20, 1981, after a group of Iranian college students belonging to the Muslim Student Followers of the Imam's Line, who supported the Iranian Revolution, took over the U.S. Embassy in Tehran.

The early 1980s recession was a severe economic recession that affected much of the world between approximately the start of 1980 and early 1983. It is widely considered to have been the most severe recession since World War Two.

It was not a good time to be unemployed as the recession from January to July 1980 kept unemployment high, and despite economic recovery, it remained at historically high levels (about 7.5%) until the end of 1981. By March 1982 unemployment had reached 9%, and by December of that year the unemployment rate stood at its recession peak of 10.8%.

Side Note:

Here's how one of the verses came out of this weird happening: At one crazy time at JW Electronics there was this giant love-tangled triangle that affected a lot of people working there. The manager, we'll just call him Mr. JC was messing around with another married woman that we'll call Mrs. L. Now when the manager's wife, that we'll call Mrs. SC, found out that her husband was running around on her, she started messing around with Mr. GE When Mr. GE's wife, Mrs. EE, heard that Mr. GE. was screwing around with Mr. JC's wife, she started making advancements and ultimately had an affair with Mr. DR. Now when Mr. DR's wife, Mrs. AR found out about her husband's infidelity she dropped him like a hot potato and got a divorce. This started a domino effect where Mr. GE got a divorce From Mrs. EE and then got married to Mrs. SC who had gotten a divorce from Mr. JC. Mr. DR. then married Mrs. EE and Mr. JC? Well, who knows what happened to Mr. JC? He certainly was not welcome by Mrs. AR.

It was in 1980 that one of the first studies of the 50-50 marriage/divorce statistics came out. So this song reflected this unhealthy marital attitude that seemed to reflect an inconsiderate selfishness along with an unwillingness to work things out, but instead, they all ended up in divorces and except for AR who was a lone victim, and GE and SC who remained married, everything eventually went south again for all the others .

By A Friend

(1986) – This song originally came out as a fluke after I had just bought a new capo for my guitar and I was singing and goofing around with Elizabeth and Meridith. I put the capo high up on the fret board and sang a goofy tune in a falsetto voice. Strangely, it sounded kind of cool so later I worked with some of the words and then wrote out the lyrics to this falsetto voice and tune. This song, about the power and potential of love and friendship, was an instant hit with Elizabeth and Meridith, in fact at one point, this was back in 1986-87, the two girls sang this song as a duet to almost all functions, family gatherings, whenever the occasion. They were well received and my only regret is that I had no way to record them and their performances back then.

Side Note:

It was a cold Wednesday morning on February 19th 1986, and it was, maybe about two in the morning when Diane got up and went into the bathroom, when her water broke. But it was cold, and instead of her waking me up to let me know that we needed to go to the hospital, (no more midwife adventures after Stephen), she went back to bed to get warm and then fell asleep. A couple hours later, maybe about 5:30 in the morning, she wakes me up excitedly, (and not in a good way), to let me know that she's having the baby. As I was going through the drill, starting to get things ready, she yells, "We need to go now! The baby is coming right now!"

I quickly woke Lori to let her know that she needed to take control and then took off. It was a clear morning as I shot out of the Evergreen Shores neighborhood, going down Black Lake Blvd. at fifty plus miles an hour with the thought that, if I was to get pulled over by the police, I could get an escort to the hospital, but, there were no police available on Black Lake Blvd. Now I'm on 101 pulling 75 mph before I get to Interstate 5 where I'm literally going 85 mph, but no police. I get to the St Peters hospital and grab a wheelchair and wheel Diane into the emergency doors. The receptionist was less than friendly, bureaucratically asking for information, until I said, "Sorry ma'am, she's having the baby right now.!"

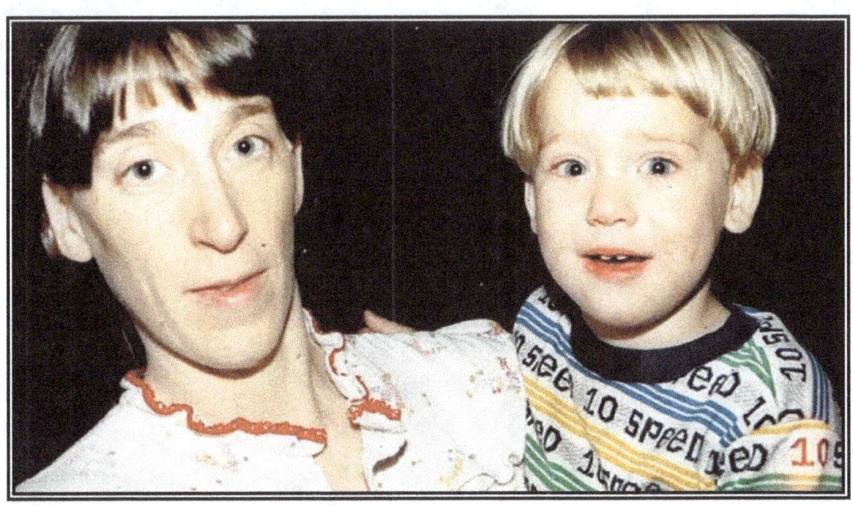

Diane with Spencer ca maybe 1989

Diane got wheeled into a small room adjacent to the emergency room as I tried to call the doctor one more time. Meanwhile the attending nurse reported that the doctor was not going to make it and that they would have to use an emergency room doctor. Five minutes later, a young man, maybe 26, came in. As he surveyed the room prior to addressing the elephant in the room, the look on his face reflected someone that did not want to be there. A nurse came in to assist and let the young doctor know that Diane was already past the second stage, and that her cervix was already fully dilated at 10 centimeters. This did not make the doctor happier though but instead grimaced as he prepared for the delivery. When the baby started to come out, the umbilical cord was wrapped around Spencer's neck. As he hesitated, I was telling the doctor how I had experienced this in the past and suggested that he might gently pull the coils off the baby's neck one by one.

The doctor took my advice and pulled the cords off from around the baby's neck. As soon as the last cord was removed, the baby, Spencer, sort of flew out and into the arms of the young doctor. As he began to clamp the umbilical cord, I said, "You know, you should wait for a couple minutes before clamping to allow any extra blood to flow from the placenta to the baby. It lowers the risk of iron-deficiency anemia. The doctor looked at the nurse who, with raised eyebrows, confirmed that what I had said was maybe true.

The young doctor then turned to me with a look of incredulousness, said, "Sir; I can have you removed."

"No you can't." I replied flippantly as he angrily turned back to Diane.

After waiting for about two minutes, he put the two clamps on, made the cut and handed the baby to the nurse who, after doing a quick clean, laid the baby on Diane's chest.

The young doctor grabbed a small plastic tub and while holding it with one hand, was pulling on the protruding umbilical cord.

I said, "you know, it's not good to pull the placenta loose from the uterus; it could cause damage to the,..."

Suddenly, the doctor took the small plastic tub and threw it on the floor causing a bloody mess on the floor, and in a huff, the doctor stormed out of the room.

The attending nurse looked at me and said, "I'm sorry." She then picked the tub back up, waited for a couple short minutes, then, pushing on the uterus, she gently pulled the placenta out by the umbilical cord.

The nurse was straightening things out, wiping the blood off of the floor as she said, "I am sorry for Dr. ? behavior."

"I'm thinking he didn't want to be here." I replied.

Fear washed over her face and I think I guessed what she was thinking.

"It's okay." I said. "It all worked out." And laughed at my unintended pun. A moment later she got the joke and laughed too.

On the way home, Diane said, "I'm never doing that again."

But later, she did; three more times; but without the heavy drama or complications.

Part Of The Plan

(1980) – This is a little difficult to explain because in fact I'm kind of torn over my feelings towards this song and what its message is. But one time, back in 1980, the thought of approaching the millennium and seeing how everything looked from a political perspective back then, this song evolved from the doomsday profiteer perspective. I think the main message that I was striving to give was that even in the last days, we need to maintain civility, love, compassion and mercy for others, as we would hope that they would give the same to us.

Yet maybe there is something more, something more to this universe and how we're all connected somehow. "Endure to the end" is a saying or phrase in the LDS church that reflects an attitude that when we're under stress and or in dire circumstances, we should continue on in the same good, kind manner, attitude and demeanor that we had or have when things are normal,

Side Note:

On March 27, 1980, a series of volcanic explosions and pyroclastic flows began at Mount St. Helens in Skamania County, Washington State. It initiated as a series of phreatic blasts from the summit.

It was a Sunday morning on May 18, 1980, there was an earthquake at about 8:30 in the morning and a couple hours thereafter, Mount St. Helens blew up. Its eruption was the deadliest and most economically destructive volcanic event in US history. Fifty-seven people were killed; 250 homes, 47 bridges, 15 miles of railways, and 185 miles of highway were destroyed. A massive debris avalanche, triggered by an earthquake of magnitude 5.1, caused a lateral eruption that reduced the elevation of the mountain's summit from 9,677 feet to 8,363 feet, leaving a 1 mile wide horseshoe-shaped crater. The debris avalanche was up to 0.7 cubic miles in volume.

I mention this because we were concerned at how powerful the volcano was and had no idea how destructive it would end up being. And it was on a Sunday, happening as we were getting ready for church. I got in my car and drove up to a high place on Delphi Road and I could see the top of the volcano and the ash spewing up into the sky. Of course, we said our prayers and as we watched it erupting on every channel, (at the time we had five channels; channel 4 (ABC), channel 5 (NBC), channel 7 (CBS), channel 9 (PBS), and channel 11, (unaffiliated at the time), we wondered what, 'part of the plan' we all were being fit into.

76

- 27 - THE NEW LOVER'S WALTZ - 1994 -

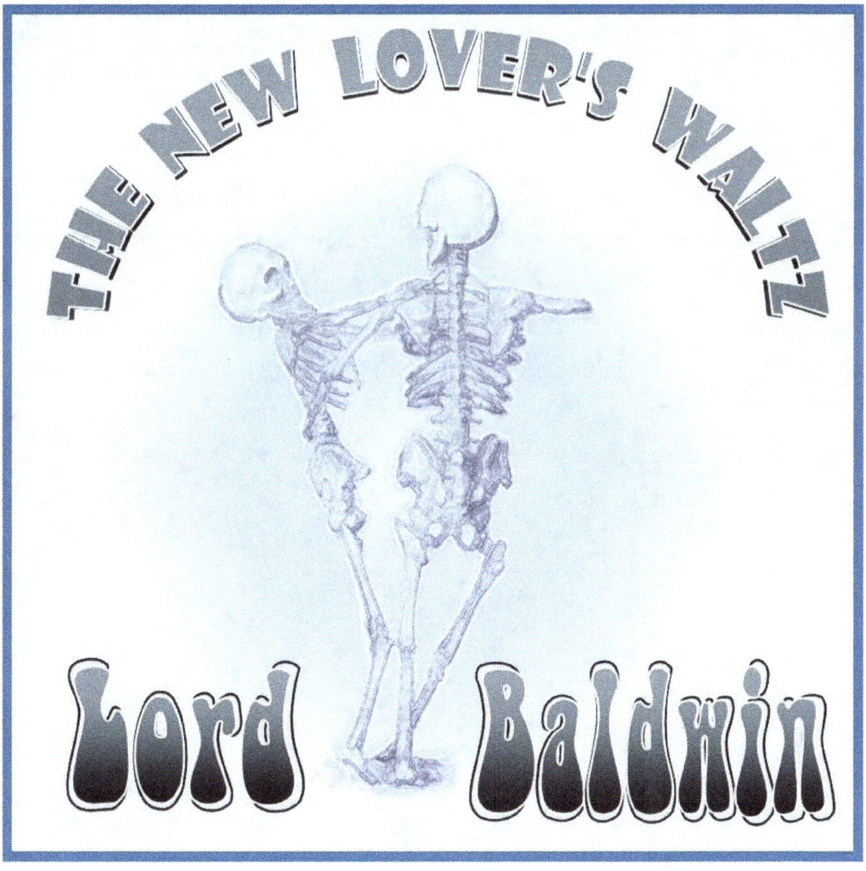

77

NOTES ABOUT THE COVERS

Notes On The New Cover:

Yeah, more dancing bones, and I had a lot to choose from, even in the public domain section. I was tempted to use a cut from Disney's, "the Skeleton Dance," but it wasn't free and I moved on. This new picture I chose from all the public domain searches I did seems to rise to the top with these elegant skeletons seemingly to be dancing a waltz. I still did my own modifications to get the picture and the lighting and colors and the lettering just right, but from the end results, I feel it all came together really well anyway.

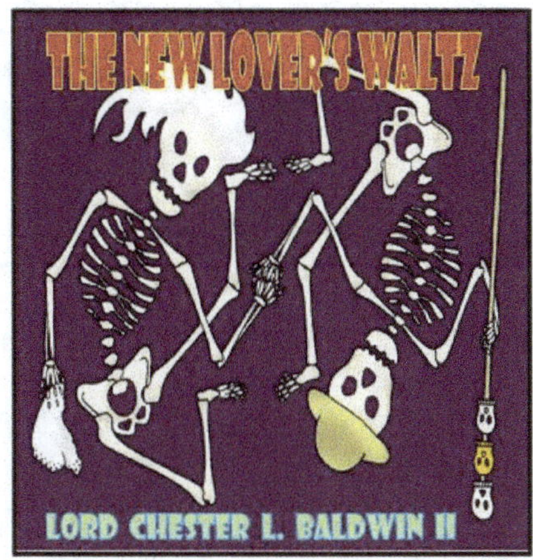

Notes On The Original Cover:

When I found these two skeletons dancing to the Mexican holiday, Cinco De Mayo, I liked how they were seemingly dancing with each other, totally devoid of time and space; I liked the hat on the male dancer the wild hair on the female, and I liked the way they seemed to fit on the cover.

The Back Cover;

a Buzbee Burkley pose with the dancers all seemingly floating in space. This was a winner, but not sure if Getty Images owns the picture so not sure I can use it

78

THE NEW LOVER'S WALTZ

79

The New Lover's Waltz

She stood there in the shadows, by the dance floor, alone,
with second thoughts, "Why did she come,
instead of staying home."
And I was afraid, unsure what to do; unsure what to do or say,
as that still, small voice whispered,
"Don't let her get away."

We might dance every dance and hum every tune.
Move in quiet time beneath the accordion moon.
Music played and lonely hearts could see beyond the faults.
We could dance forever to, "The New Lover's Waltz."

I followed her, she looked at me but I couldn't find my voice,
yet something drew us closer
till we had to make the choice.
I couldn't speak I couldn't think but she wouldn't wait anymore.
She took my hand and took my lead
as we circled round the floor.

And we danced every dance and hummed every tune,
moving in perfect time beneath the accordion moon.
Music played as new hearts swayed beyond those ballroom walls.
We should dance forever to, "The New Lover's Waltz."

As the time goes by and with each new problem that we face,
together and alone
we're still dancing in place.
And we dance the joys and sorrows that come with each day,
and we dance this life forever
in our own special way.

We have danced every dance; hummed every tune,
moved in three-four time beneath the accordion moon.
Music plays and true hearts sway as love eternal calls.
We will dance forever to, "The New Lover's Waltz."

80

What Will You Do?

What will you do when they come back at you?
They don't like your voice and they've given you the choice,
that you change it or you leave, find another trick up your sleeve.
You don't feel like singing the blues; what will you do?

What will you say when they throw you off the stage?
Tear your poetry apart; down to the very last page.
You've got to find escape or get punched in the face,
western songs seem out of place, what will you say?

What will you feel with a ticket for a meal?
Singing songs so real with no one listening to kneel.
There is no medicine to heal and you're almost down to steal,
as your rock and roll won't wheel, What will you feel?

Where will you go when you run out of the road?
You've sang out all your soul, changing winds outside are cold.
All your promises are sold and your stories still untold,
as the folk scene starts to mold, where will you go?

81

Just Another Bimmy - No. 2

I walk into town after escaping the hounds.
A vagrant out of jail with the county on my tail.
A tapped city jerk and looking for work.
I enter the back door like a hundred times before.

As my desperation shows they all think my life is low.
So I'm working any take; and I'm waiting for a break.
Bussing tables, mopping floors,
washing windows, painting doors;

I'm just another Bimmy, from another city.

Trying to find a better way but all I get's another bus tray.
Doing what I hate; washing silverware and plates.
Sorting through knishes just to find my dishes.
Scrubbing scalding hot pans and burning my hands.

Dreaming of you and me, and how I thought it would be.
Selling shoes on the street trying to make ends meet.
Singing the staff quarters blues; either way I lose.

I Come in early; I stay here late. I work so hard for so little pay;

I'm just another Bimmy, from another city.

A day late and dollar short, half sick from too much port.
No worries, no debts; no friends, no regrets.
Sorting through the trash for some extra cash.
Every man must measure his own kind of treasure.

Fly by night and slip away; thumb a ride to another state.

I enter the back door like a hundred times before.
As my desperation shows they all think my life is low.
And you know it's a pity when you're getting all gritty,
but far from free, or where I should be;

I'm just another Bimmy, from another city.
I'm just another Bimmy, from another city.

82

This Time

Away, as quick as we can go, and maybe if we don't move too slow
we can make it before she burns,
before the mob outside turns,
they're all reaching for returns,
but violence never learns.

Today; crew boss up at Creeks Bend
said the diggings are all going to end.
And the mine's closed up today. This panic is like a fire in the hay.
This town has no other way than that pick and shovel pay.

This time; we're really gonna feel it, yes.
This time; we may not heal it, no. This time; it'll die.

And now; the day speaks for itself; not a can was left on any shelf,
when the supermarket and the banks were blown,
when the insecurity seeds were sown,
when no consideration for the laws were shown,
and the number of dead in the streets unknown.

This time; we're really gonna feel it, yes.
This time; we may not heal it, no. This time; it'll die.

Oh, the night; so cold and yet so warm;
darkness keeping us from the storm.
Behind us we can see it burn,
and what did anybody learn?

Today it broke, everyone everywhere awoke,
like some horrible joke; or some past words spoke.

This time; we're really gonna feel it, yes.
This time; we may not heal it, no. This time; it'll die.

83

Go Get Her

She stands behind the counter at the little convenience store.
The smiles and hellos excite me to the core.
I want to take the chance but I'm too afraid to ask,
so the silence in reserve is worn for a mask.

I think about the future, but feel awkward and inept.
I want her in my life but it's hard to take the first step.
I want to go get her, just like I've dreamed.
Anything too easily gained is too little esteemed.

Hey, I wanna go get her, before it's too late.
We're both looking for love but she might not wait.

She's made a move, broken the ice and the questions start to fly,
she tells me of her life and the pleasantries go by.
She asks about my passions as I try to play it cool.
but I fumble with the words and I feel I've been a fool.

I know the time is now but I pause for fear instead,
my senses scream to ask as the voices in my head;

they say, go get her just like I've dreamed.
Anything too easily gained is too little esteemed.

Go on; go get her before it's too late;
we're both looking for love but she might not wait.

Go get her just like I've dreamed.
Anything too easily gained is too little esteemed.

I want to go get her before it's too late;
we're both looking for love but she might not wait.

84

The Meaning of My Life

I was sad, for the shape of things that are;
disappointed with my station so far.
Seems there's no time to better what I could be;
seems like I've failed all my family's needs.
hard times and trials are always right behind
but the happiness and peace are just a state of mind.

It's a point of view; an attitude. It's what I make with what I do.
How much I learn and love through my wrong and right.
With less to take and more to give, in all the days I have to live,
I think I'm close to the meaning of my life.

There comes a time, we need to look around,
see what we can do with the needs that we've found.
How can we whine with a heart that bleeds,
while there's so many that have so many greater needs.
Hard times and trials will always be my lot,
but things will get better with every day, I'm not.

It's a point of view, and an attitude, it's what I make with what I do.
How much I learn and love through wrong and right.
With less to take and more to give, in all the days I have to live
I think I'm close to the meaning of my life.

They don't want money or a clever line;
they just need a little of your time.
So many in need of a helping hand;
it's time for me and you to make that stand.

It's a point of view and an attitude, it's what I make with what I do.
How much I learn and love through wrong and right.
With less to take and more to give, in all the days I have to live
I get myself closer to the meaning of my life.

The purpose all comes in full view
when we realize how much we can do.
A hand held out to touch that soul;
a smile of thankfulness is all we need to know.

It's a point of view and an attitude, it's what I make with what I do.
How much I learn and love through wrong and right.
With less to take and more to give; in all the days I have to live
I know I'm finding the meanings of my life.

85

Plans To Keep

Unemployed, paranoid as opportunities fall away.
Ceilings descend, walls close in and I'm trapped without escape.
Climbing hills and paying bills with wolves pacing out the door.
They're looking for me, it's no mystery, I know what they're waiting
for.

But I've got plans to keep, and I've got dreams to breach.
I can't let this setback influence what I want to do,
no, I've got a vision and a dream that I'll make come true.

They all say, "Someday," as the "here and now" softly numbs.
Architecture for failure; it's the tomorrow that never comes.
The hidden fears of later years, unthought of while in good health.
Lamented wails, forsaken tales as "it's too late to do anything else."

Yet I've got plans to keep, and I've got dreams to breach.
I can't let this setback influence what I want to do;
I've got a vision, a dream that I'll make come true.

They're out there in force, waiting till that time arrives.
They make it a sport to break down and destroy other lives.
I've no need for them, I won't offer my hand for them to bite,
as they carry away my good dreams into a foreboding night.

Unemployed, paranoid but I'll pull myself out of these holes.
Shrugging doubts; looking out to keep focused on my goals.
Climbing hills, strengthening wills, learning on new paths I tread
Reevaluate and calculate, an eye single to the task ahead.

But I've got plans to keep, and I've got dreams to breach.
I can't let this setback influence what I want to do,
I've got a vision, a dream that I'll make come true.

86

⸎

MEMOIRS & NOTES - 27 - 'THE NEW LOVER'S WALTZ'

The New Lover's Waltz

(1991) – This song was written during a half-hour lunch break after the tune came to my head, while I was working on a computer earlier that morning at the Washington State Parks. I was swaying back and forth as envisioned this melodic piece as the words themselves danced with the waltzing music; my favorite line, *"moved in 3-4 time beneath the accordion moon."*

It was all reminiscent of those childhood days when I went to the Swing Fests, or to be sure; Schwingfests which encompasses, Schwingen, also known as Swiss wrestling, (which is considered the "national sport" of Switzerland), and in the afternoon, Steinstossen, (Stone Throwing), where a huge boulder was picked up and thrown  as far as the man could throw it.

At night, the atmosphere changed as German – Swiss food was served and afterwards, there were special Swiss deserts and for the protein lovers, there was always an abundance of cervelats; the national sausage of Switzerland that are traditionally packed into zebu or humped cattle's intestines, then slightly smoked and then boiled. As the kids are eating deserts and sausages, the dancing to polka music begins, while many of the adults are drinking beer and a lot of it. To this day, whenever I smell someone smoking a cigar, I'm reminded of the Swing Fests I went to when I was younger. It just said something to me and motivated me to continue writing the rest of this song.

Side Note:

All through my childhood I was infatuated with the sound of accordions and later on, the ambience of polka music; I am finding and evolving with the love of that sound; it is just happy music to me.

But a revelation and realization came to me years later when I moved back in with my dad; the comprehension that it was all from him—it was from his accordion playing when I was a small child that influenced me to gravitate to harmonica and ultimately to help shape my musical heart and soul.

My dad in the early 50s

What Will You Do?

(1974) – There was a time in 1974 where I made great attempts to do something with this talent I had, never mind the fact that I had a very small repertoire, and I reached out to the musical community and did a lot of open mikes, soliciting of my material to record companies and radio stations all with little to no success. That moment I told you about earlier, where I went into a bar to audition for a talent manager and promoter, who promised to meet me at a particular tavern on SE Hawthorne Blvd. (changed over in 1983 to McMenamin's Barley Mill Pub) to see and hear my stuff.

I need to say that when I went into the bar to play there that night, I was scared. I was scared of the neighborhood that I was walking through in the dark with my guitar in hand, I was scared of the redneck crowd that permeated this tavern at the time, but most of all, I was scared of failure and screwing up on my big chance to success.

So, I went in there, had a few glasses of pop, and while I waited for this gut to show up, listened to the other talent that mostly played one or two songs. I was holding back, thinking maybe the guy was late, but unfortunately, the manager promoter never seemed to show up or make himself known, and I figured as the evening went on that maybe he was indeed there, hiding out in the crowd to see how I might do on my own. And I was uncomfortable sitting there with all these people progressively getting more drunk as the evening pressed on.

Now I believe that there are three main categories that users of alcohol fall into; 1, the social drinker, 2, the alcohol abuser or 3, the alcoholic. Most people who drink alcohol will not have any problems with their consumption; however, for those who do have a problem handling it, oftentimes, their problem will gradually worsen and can get ugly very quickly. And in any bar on any given Friday of Saturday night, you might have an equal amount of all three, which, in the end, could even things out for me. And I never was one to do covers of other's material, and there are always those in bars that can be really hard to deal with if they don't like what you're doing.

Towards the end of the open mike session, I got up on that stage and gave, what I believed to be, a flawless performance of, "Lonely Too Long." It was well received so I broke into, "Stealing Away Again." I was ready to go but the crowd yelled for more and I finished with, "Something Must Be Wrong." After I finished, and was packing up my guitar, I looked out at the people sitting at the bar and at the different tables, but I couldn't tell which one might be the promoter. Still, I was well received and so the promoter would have to have been impressed.

On my walk home from that evening I wondered what I would have done if things hadn't gone the way they did. And I thought about a lot of different scenarios and how I might have reacted to each of them from the different perspectives heretofore mentioned, like if I was singing the blues to some regular country and western audience, or doing hard rock and roll to the folk music people, (look what happened to Dylan at the Newport Folk Festival in 1965). In a way, the results could have all ended up being the same, but then, if they didn't like my material, things could have gone south very quickly.

By the time I got home I had most of the lyrics and the tune already down in my head. It was late and Diane was asleep so I went into the kitchen, cut myself a piece of her apple pie and proceeded to start writing down the lyrics. Diane came in with sleepy eyes asking how the performance went. After I told her all the details, she was decidedly angry, which of course made me feel good because it not only showed that she understood my pain but that she believed in me and my songs. And so, even though it was a sad moment, it was an opportunity for me to get a feel for what others thought of my material. And, let's face it, it was a memorable moment for me.

Side Note:

The Chinese Castle was, in fact, a duplex. The left stairs led to the bottom floor, and the stairs to the right, was the second-floor apartment. Imagine if you will, the building was painted in a bright yellow with a reddish-orange trim.

The Chinese Castle

Being the second-floor apartment, we also had use of the entire attic that spanned the whole building, minus the curved ceiling. The basement was cordoned off with a wall down the middle where we had the right side and the first floor had the left side.

There was also a shared space where the washer and dryer were. When Grandma Scarbrough passed away in November, (on the same day and maybe eight hours before Lori was born), she left a lot of stuff; good stuff, old stuff that after my mother took care of the arrangements, had me take and put into the basement. I won't go into all the 30 years of stuff that went down there but there was a lot of good stuff.

Diane and I had met the neighbors downstairs; a family of two kids, eight months apart, with another to be born eight months after the last baby) and I had spoken with the father, a young man that was unemployed and not really interested in going to work. Instead, he had ideas of getting rich quick and without having a strong ethical background, sound principles or moralities, was talking about doing illegal things.

One day I came home and found the family had moved out. It

wasn't that same day, but later I went into the basement and found my neighbor had broken down the door in between the two sides and stole much of my Grandma Scarbrough's treasures.

And if you've been following me and these memoirs, you might remember me mentioning my wonderful Christmas present from 1967; my treasured, EL-3302 - 'Philips' *Play and Record Portable Cassette Deck.*

The EL-3302 was a mono com-pact cassette recorder made by the Philips Company in 1967. Manu-factured to a mass volume and produced in many countries, the majority of the earlier units came from Austria. This was a player and recorder, with built in erase bias for a separate erase head pro-viding high quality audio reproduction from compact cassettes. It has a full range of tape control features including fast-forward, rewind, and play. The pause function was a switch on the microphone, which simply cut the power to the motor.

Anyway, that neighbor stole that too, which was a big loss to me, but inside the recorder was my one and only copy of my earliest recordings of my work, including, "*A Salute To Mr. Zigzag.*" I would have been glad to have had him steal my recorder, (not really) if he had just left my cassette tape,... I still lament its loss.

Just Another Bimmy (No. 2)

(1971-77) – As you may remember from my album, "Taking Me For A Ride," I recorded a song called, "Just Another Bimmy" which was written in 1971 by my brother Richard. It was about his experiences as a dishwasher in a small restaurant Ice Cream Parlor called, "Charlou's" in Monticello New York. The derogatory term, Bimmy came out of the late 50s and early 60s denoting immigrant Puerto Ricans and Cubans along with many people of color from the city, ("the City" was a term used for New York City by anyone withing a 200 mile radius of NYC), that worked in the resort hotels in the kitchens, did general cleaning, washing dishes or did any type of menial an monotonous work. In the middle of the 60s, the term Bimmy took on a new meaning denoting or including and Caucasian persons working in those lowlife jobs. Richie, who had taken this lowlife job at Charlou's, washing dishes and bussing tables, had become a Bimmy himself. While working there Richie wrote most of the words to this song in 1971.

I took Richie's poem and elaborated on this work in 1977. I took the words and embellished them and included much of my own then put music to the words. After Richard heard my version, he decided to take a few of my ideas and incorporate them into his own work.

This later version has the protagonist leaving the kitchen of Charlou's and finds this person, a vagrant and destitute with problematic circumstances as he travels from town to town and job to job.

This Time

(1970) – I think this may be the first guitar song I ever wrote. I bought this wonderful 12-string Yamaha guitar that had such a wonderful sound. Back then, to learn how to play the guitar and become skilled at where my fingers needed to be for the different cords, I would compose music for a song using chords that I knew I couldn't play at all, or at least not very well. This would challenge my ability as I would struggle through that chord progression to improve my fingering. The music for, "This Time," was written in the key of "C" and I traversed back and forth from "C" to "F" as the melody and the words went on in the song. I would sit for hours, just going back and forth from "C" to "F" until my fingers would say, "no more." And because I did not have calluses, my fingers bled. Still, I knew that there was a price to pay for learning to play a guitar and I was willing to pay that price if I could only become good enough to get past the sounds of rubber bands. (That was a term Diane used to describe the sound that she made when I was teaching her how to play the guitar). I was living out in the country in White Plains, New York, in a double bungalow with John, David, Richie and Charlie, (and Bobby Adler; more on him maybe later), all of whom avoided me and my guitar noise as much as possible. This is one of the only songs that I wrote and played on that Yamaha guitar before that fateful day months later when someone stole it from my Kingston apartment when I moved back to Portland.

Side Note:

The Farmington Mine disaster happened on November 20, 1968, at the Consol No. 9 Coal Mine, north of Farmington, West Virginia.

There was an explosion that happened at approximately 5:30 a.m. The explosion was large enough to be felt in Fairmont, almost 12 miles away. At the time, 99 miners were inside. Over the course of the next few hours, 21 miners were able to escape the mine, but 78 were still trapped. All who were unable to escape perished; the bodies of 19 of the dead were never recovered. The cause of the explosion was never positively determined, but the accident served as the catalyst for several new laws that were passed to protect miners. The news on

The Farmington Mine Disaster - November 20, 1968

the radio a year and a half later reported that the town of Farmington was having a hard time recovering from the tragedy. I wrote this song to commemorate this happening.

Go Get Her

(1993) – This all came from a simple phrase, "Go Get Her" and I elaborated on the idea that there she is, you want her, you think you need her, and go get her.

This piece was a lot of fun to create. I start with the percussion as this unsettling organ music is in the shadows then a roll and a wild harmonica doing a double time to the drum and then the singer starts singing. And then there's a pause, (one of a few) then the singer comes back and reminds us of the urgency to move it or lose it. (Go Get Her) then another verse, pause, then the return of 40 seconds of that wild harmonica playing double time, (in the key of "C" I believe) until, abruptly, I just kind of stop everything and the song ends. This was not the way I had envisioned the ending of this song, and even after the song had been recorded, I was going to come back. But in early April, I realized that I hadn't put out any new music for four or five months and then went into a kind of rush mode when I went to engineer albums 27 and 28, (I think I may have mentioned before, when I put together the music, I was doing them two at a time, each 45-minutes or less so as to be able to fit on a 90-minute cassette) and I recorded it the way it is here. And yes, I was going to come back for a reengineered version but it never happened.

Side Note: In 1993 Chet was working at McDonalds on the west side of Olympia. He had a company of friends from there, many of them were also members of the church, but in other wards; mostly the Olympia Second. Aside from the fact that all of them were teenagers, some of them had licenses to drive and some even had their own cars. And there was a thing at the time where they would go cruising after work. Chet, not having a car at the time would often borrow our car.

At the time we had a 1980 Ford Escort Station Wagon that we bought for $500.00. Its previous owner was a large person whose weight had eventually broken the driver's front seat on one side making the driver sit catawampus when they were going down the road.

One day I was driving the car to work and I noticed the steering was a bit off and there seemed to be a small wobble coming from the rear tires. I took it to Les Schwab after work and they assured me that the tires were fine. Maybe two weeks later Diane was driving the car to Black Lake Elementary School when the car suddenly froze up. I traded the body of the car and paid my friend Marty Petkovich $400.00 and got a 1975 AMC Hornet. (Maybe more about the hornet later).

Fast forward and seven years later the family was all sitting around maybe Christmas time, and I heard a story about one night at McDonalds years earlier where they, (the teenagers we talked about earlier), after work at 1:30 in the morning and they were out in the parking lot driving around, more like screwing around, practicing this thing with their cars called "drifting," which is a driving technique where the driver intentionally oversteers, with loss of traction, while maintaining control, usually using the emergency stick brake, and then driving the car on through the entirety of a corner. And apparently the Escort had a pretty good emergency brake so they were having a lot of fun until one of the drifts slammed the right side back tire into one of the concrete parking blocks. They did notice there was a slight wobble but thought it would be okay. But I was never told that story. Made me wonder how many other incidents happened with other kids that I may never know or it will come out at some family gathering. By the way, most of this group of Chet's have remained loyal friends to this day.

The Meaning Of My Life

(1993) – Looking at what I do and why and finding purpose in it all. The words to this song were random thoughts and ideas that I had put down on paper in hopes of giving me ideas to harvest at a later date and write many other songs. I took the challenge one afternoon to create a song using all these random ideas. This turned out different than what I started with.

Over the years, the idea of what was important to me as well as the meaning of my life played a huge part in my own thought processes. Much of this had to do with looking at my role as a parent and husband. It was a time to contemplate what the world might look like if I had not had as many children as I did, but moreover, the good that I instilled in them might snowball or have the domino effect for future generations to come. It's also an inherent time to consider what the world looks like from each of my children's eyes. And with so many from so many ages and perspectives, this was a daunting task. And I saw the way things were for me, my successes and failures and in comparison, to what I believed should have been. That is a slippery slope there, that comparing thing; for we don't know about the might have been; we don't know if, even in the most perfect scenarios whether things would end up like we think they will. And I concluded that indeed, it's all a point of view; mine and yours are bound to not be the same, and that comparing thing can be altered or controlled by our attitude.

If I see myself from the perspective of today, it's really not the same as someone, like yourself, who is reading these words and knowing that guy; that Lord Baldwin; reading his words, listening to his songs, figuring out that it was what he made with what he did, with what he had available, from mistakes and how much he learned and hopefully, how much he gave of his time and energy to his family, and in all the days he had to live, maybe he did get closer to the meaning of his life.

And sure, there comes a time, we all need to look around; see what we can do for our neighbors, our friends, our enemies, looking for the needs that they have, the problems we might be able to fix.

I realized that there are two aspects to consider when pondering the meaning of life. There's the meaning of life to us individually and then the meaning of life for humanity, or the idea of interconnectedness to us to our families and generations to come. I thought about how beliefs in intelligent design gives meaning to many people's lives. I am LDS; a member of the Church of Jesus Christ of Latter-Day Saints, and I believe in the importance of being kind and charitable and loving.

When evaluating the meaning of my life, I think I need to consider what makes me happy, and these things, these situations, and all these people in my life, all of these things are what give my life meaning. As I continue on my own individual passage toward realizing the meaning of my life, the creation of music, the writing of poems, the transforming of such into songs, this is what makes me happy, but I do these things for and in behalf of my family, for I am truly happiest when I feel that connection of me being a part of and together with my family.

Plans To Keep

(1993) – The majority of the words for this song were written during the time I was unemployed at the beginning of 1992. I found these depressing words scribbled down on a pad and tucked away in a bunch of my Boy Scout stuff. It was not hard to relate to the unhappiness and uncertainty of being unemployed while carrying such a large responsibility of nine children. Because I was employed by the time that I rewrote this tune, I was a little more optimistic and I added the middle eight, "I've got plans to keep" stanza to give a sense of hope in all the despair. In some respects, I kind of feel like I should've left the song alone, but I had gone through so much depression over the last year that I didn't want to perpetuate that downer feeling.

Over the years I have found that the eating of the elephant, one bite at a time is achievable. I have been driven to keep pushing forward, even in the face of adversity and failure. I know that other trials will come; other lessons will need to be learned, that's just the way of life. Taking stock in my steps, reveling in my small accomplishments and advancements instead of feeling a sense of being defeated, and that's so important. Don't worry about the endgame when I'm still in the middle trying to go forward.

I have found that there are four keys to success;

1,... Decide exactly what I want to convey and where I'm gonna want to go with this.

2,... Set a deadline and make a plan to get there, but don't get discouraged when it takes longer than I expected or planned.

3,... Take action on my plan; do something every day (write every day, play music every day), to help myself to move toward my goal.

4,... Resolve in advance that I will continue to persist until I succeed.

5,... Determine and resolve that I will never, ever give up.

And when problems do come up. I get discouraged at times, but I can't let those setbacks dictate my behavior in a negative way. to prevent me from what I want to do and impact my progress, however slim it may be. I know from experience that that kind of mindset will only make things worse me. And so I try to keep my eyes on the vision or goal with my simple, fleeting dream, and if I can just stay focused and keep working on it, I may make that dream come true after all.

87

- 28 - ON THE EDGE OF A VERY STRANGE LIGHT

88

NOTES ABOUT THE COVERS

Notes On The New Covers:

Okay, this cover is a trip. Even if you don't have the inkling of seeing faces in everything, there are maybe, seven different faces in there somewhere and, I envision a kind of, portal to time traveling in the center of the circle.

And there's a faerie lizard under the "a" and,... well, you go ahead and see if you can find some of the other hidden images,...

Notes On The Original Covers:

Surprised? Yes this used to have a whole different album name. And look, right? I was going for a kind of gothic shade and you'll notice the arrangement and positions of songs are different. And the back cover was kind of trippy with ghostly images.

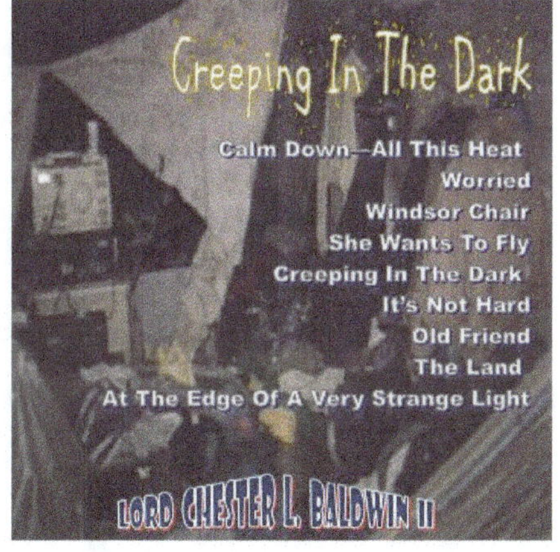

89

ON THE EDGE OF A VERY STRANGE LIGHT

On The Edge Of A Very Strange Light
Old Friend
It's Not Hard
She Wants To Fly Away
Worried
Windsor Chair

90

On The Edge Of A Very Strange Light

Standing at the edge of a very strange light,
conceived in love and died in hate.
God has set his wheels to roll; the madness might decide his fate.
Elusively I watched him change,
he strives to be the god here on earth.
He gathers all possessions he can store,
with no real concern of its worth.
I can't communicate with him, he's isolated all the truth.
He's forced the restoration to decay,
without a clear knowledge of what to do.
He leaves no water, destroys his own air.
He's taken my land to build his wall.
And he takes and he breaks with no thoughts of mistakes
and no contemplation of tomorrow's fall.
Man has done this to himself,
immortality dreams lead this nightmare game.
The dream once shared is now dissolved,
he's only himself, not the times to blame.

91

Old Friend

Old Friend, where did we go? Far beyond our reach, to teach.
Old Friend, where are we now? Far beyond our turn, to learn?
Old Friend, where did you go?
I thought you'd be right back
when you found your lack.

Old Friend, where are you now? Long and far away, from me today.
Letters get harder to write, hoping you'll never lose sight.
Traveling the fly by night to the temporary home, always alone.

Old Friend, where did I go? Nowhere; never away, always the same.
Old Friend, where am I now? Long and far away, and yet I stay.
Library window at dawn,
all of my treasures are gone.
You are what keeps me on; I still wait by your gate.

Old Friends never die, just because they're gone, they live on.
Old Friends never die, save those that never give, never live.

92

It's Not Hard

It's not hard to be contentious while mistakes surround us all,
and it's easy to be rude to some
while labeling their faults.

But it's hard to reason thoughtfully, under stress construed.
It's so hard to forgive rudeness
but you gain love when you do.

When you do unto others who need your help.
When you do unto others as yourself.

It's not hard to be sarcastic, pushing words so anguish grows.
Tearing down a foe
that just might benefit from all you know.

But it's hard to have compassion for that neighbor round the bend,
who is hung up with his problems
and could really use a friend.

When you do unto others who need your help.
When you help other people as yourself you'll soon know
all your problems won't seem all that bad
when shared with other folks.

It's not hard to lose perspectives,
where you are from where you've been.
Always judging and comparing
you and yours with other men.

But it's hard to live life humble, know you're unique from everyone,
You've your own self to compete with
and your own prize to be won.

When you do unto others as yourself.
When you do unto others that need your help.

When you do unto others
as you would have others do unto you.

93

She Wants To Fly

It's morning, she hesitates to move,
with so much of yesterday to catch up to.
It's a struggle to get herself in the groove.
She doesn't feel he cares about the truth.

He walks into the kitchen with a smile,
expecting the breakfast that she's made.
Still in silence he eats in his usual style,
and with a few words and his lunch, he goes away.

And she wonders, "What am I doing here?"
"Why do I let this empty life go on?"
She knows she's reached her saddest fear,
a relationship where most of the love is gone.

She wants to be, so high and so free,
from all the weights and strings.
She wants to fly away, into the night,
till the morning sun touches her wings.

The afternoon; so humid and gray,
she hangs the laundry out to dry.
And she daydreams of places far away,
and wonders why she has to live this lie.

A flock of geese wing overhead somewhere,
as she yearns for the freedom of the skies.
Is there really happiness for her out there,
or is it just a prison in disguise?

As she works on the obvious, the things in sight,
contemplating running off to something new,
still between the hopes and fears of flight,
she sadly doesn't know what she should do.

She wants to be, so high and so free,
from all the weights and strings.
She wants to fly away, into the night,
till the morning sun touches her wings.

94

Worried

I worry for the future of ecology's lot.
I worry about why, and I worry why not.
I worry about my children; do they get enough?
I worry about my children; do they get too much?

Well, I'm worried, worried, worried, worried.
Yes, I'm worried about the time that moves too fast,
I'm worried about the present catching up with my past.
I worry my teeth and my hair falling out,
I worry about our food with all these chemicals about;

and I worry, worry; I worry, worry.

Got to stop, too much stress to take.
Always dwelling in doubt is a big mistake.
Got to stop being a worry slave,
or I'll worry myself to an early grave.

I'm worried about the economy falling into the night,
I worry about the leaders doing what's right.

I worry about my friends and how they might be,
I worry about my friends and what they think of me,
and I worry; worry.

I worry about the air with every breath,
and I'm worried about life and I worry about death.
I'm worried; did my life have something to tell?
I worry about heaven and I'm worried about hell,

and I'm worried, worried, worried, worried.

Got to stop, too much stress to take.
Always dwelling in doubt is a big mistake.
Got to stop being a worry slave,
or I'll worry myself to an early grave.

Got to stop, too much stress to take.
Always dwelling in doubt is a big mistake.
Got to stop being a worry slave,
or I'll worry myself to an early grave.

95

Windsor Chair

It's been over a year; things have quieted down here.
I wonder how the city is for you.
I keep busy in my dreams, but the cold reality,
is I'm lost without a plan of what to do.

Everyone's moved away, after that fateful day.
Just a few have lingered on from necessity,
so, I'm waiting for some call, with work for us all;
each day is an exercise in futility.

Articles and treasures fill this house my father built.
I will not leave this heritage even as the county wilts.
The home, the land, the family history is there,
so, I sit and gaze outside from my Windsor chair.

The vacant shops and posts are inhabited by ghosts.
The wind moans softly through the empty streets.
With no money to disperse, things went from bad to worse;
the government has asked us all to leave.

Still my life and past remain, I'm too old to ride the train;
there's just a few of us that persist to question why.
I'm waiting for the call, that will change things for us all;
tell the truth; really, are we all doomed to die?

Articles and memories filled this home from far and near.
I can not return my back to all I hold and love so dear.
Destruction of the world may come and go, I don't care.
I'll watch it come to pass, here, from my Windsor chair.

96

MEMOIRS & NOTES - 28 -
'ON THE EDGE OF A VERY
STRANGE LIGHT'

On The Edge Of A Very Strange Light

(1970) – When I was 14, I was in an empty lot next to the Belle Acres Trailer Park digging in the field for phosphorous veins. I'm with my sometimes friend Rory who arguably was letting me do all the work of digging multiple holes in the dark.

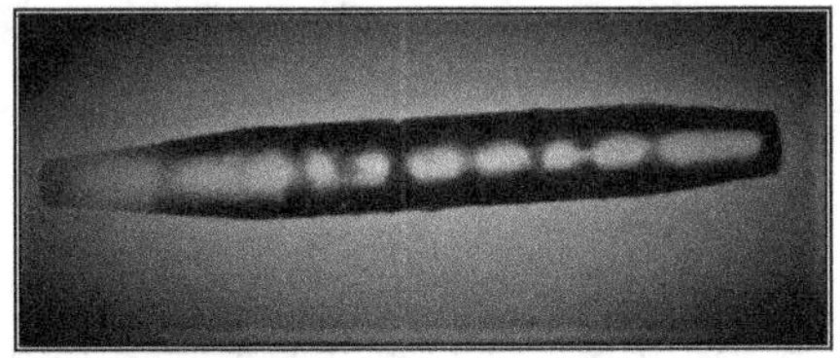

Then it happened. Up in the LA night skies was this array of multiple lights (windows?) shining brightly, reflecting a cigar-like shaped object that was hovering up in the black night.

Yes, Rory reminded me that it was probably a military transport helicopter, but I told Rory that I didn't think that they had ten to twelve windows to them, and even if they did, I pointed out that it would have to be a huge helicopter and that there was no sound whatsoever and if this was a newer, larger-than-usual military transport helicopter we'd certainly be able to hear something. Then, after being stationary for about two minutes, it moved. And it moved vertically up so quickly and then hovered there. "Did you see that?" I asked Rory, who I knee had, because I scanned his surprised face as it moved. Rory said nothing. Then, as if to be teasing us further, it seemed to move closer to us where we could see the light of it was indeed a length of bright lights separated by dark spaces. Still no sound. Then the object started to rise and move up and away from us at what had to be, incredible speed, and within the span of about ten seconds it moved up and away to become a single light that looked like a star amongst the other stars, and then its light dimmed and disappeared. Rory and I talked about that for weeks, but after a while after Rory had met up with skepticism from others, he started to doubt. But I never will forget what I saw, and whatever it was, UFO or not, it was not something someone can explain away so easily. And nonetheless, I am a believer.

Side Note:

An awareness of our surroundings is good to have in life, but a change in attitude is essential. Here is another one of my very early guitar songs, written in that bungalow in upstate New York. The idea of this song deals with how an outsider (alien from another planet?) might, after seeing some of the overbearing political structures like the still seething heap of the fractured Republican party caused of late from the fallout of the Nixon administration; their need to prove spending should be kept at a minimum so the real spoils and money gleaned from the overtaxed middle class American could be administered to projects, programs and hidden slush funds that would benefit the Republican leaders rather than their constituents. Meanwhile on important issues of the poor and weak civil rights and stifled inequality, ironically hurting the folks living in the red states that superfluously and naïvely voted them in power. Repeatedly putting off the needs and wants of their own poor and People Of Colour, they instead in their powered selfishness, remain immovable or intractable, and through corruption called lobbying, line their pockets with the wealth of the United States. Even as kindnesses are stripped away, moving altruism towards their own humanity backwards from with a kind of attitude of insatiability and greed.

Another Side Note:

And now, we see the fruits of that attitude coming to pass as we ignore scientists and experts telling us that there's a problem with the ozone,

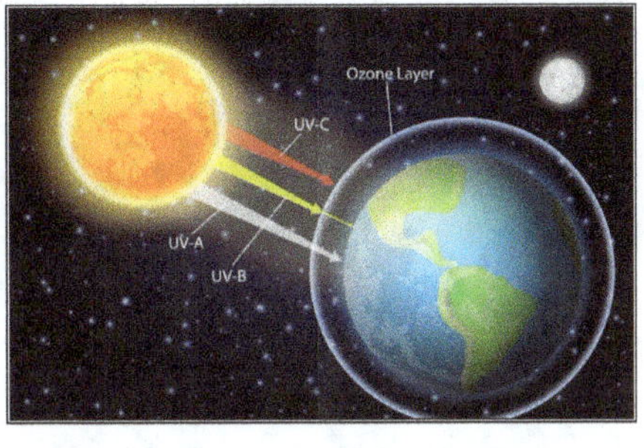

and with global warming, and with our delicate environment, the pollutioning of our oceans, the killing off of endangered species and the clear cutting and deforestation of our rain forests around the world; and all done with lit-tle regard to anything or anyone except the consumption and accumulation of more money, of swelling power and an unrighteous dominion to, not just the United States, but to the rest of our fragile world and to us, our children and our children's children.

Old Friend

(1966-68) – We moved out of Clarence's apartment and into this house after mother got a job, yet again as a **Chuck Wagon Food Truck Driver**.

(Maybe more on that later). This song found its beginning on an old piano in the basement of a three-story house in the Westmoreland section of Portland Oregon in in 1966.

By this time school started and I was going to Cleveland High School, and after football practice, I had to use my time wisely as my primary duty after school was to take care of Grandpa Scarbrough, and then make sure that Richie had dinner made, and then to make sure everyone did their homework, and then get my own homework done.

House in Westmoreland Portland Oregon

And there was my general responsibility to watch over Richie, Charlie and Mary and make sure they were all safe and that they didn't cause trouble with one another.

And after all that, I would go down into the cement basement; (in that picture, that doorway on the right leading from the sidewalk, was a private door to the basement). Inside that basement was this really old but really cool foot-pump player piano. And scattered in multiple boxes were a large assortment of piano rolls.

First, let me say, I knew nothing about this magnificent beast when we first got there, and the billows to the foot-pump part of the player piano did not work. I knew nothing of the mechanics to this beast, but, as my time allowed, in between all the other things I needed to do, and I disassembled the whole thing, studied the insides, found out that the foot-petal billows had gotten disconnected.

After a lot of hours dinking with the piano, reconnecting the billows, and putting it back together the way I thought it should be, surprisingly, it worked. The first roll I put on was, '*Clair de Lune*,' a piece from French composer named *Claude Debussy*. As I pumped away with my feet the tune filled the basement with beautiful music.

I was so excited over my triumph that I ran upstairs and brought my mother down to hear. Of course, everyone else trailed behind her. As I was playing the piano roll, my mother smiled in delight and told me that that song was her favorite music in the world. (It was the one and only music played at her funeral in 1996). Mother then took command of the piano and played a few more rolls before we all went upstairs and to bed.

I don't believe my mother ever came back down there in that basement again,... but from those other piano rolls, I discovered a treasure trove of music from some great composers as well as some early 20th century artists, like, '*Someone's Rocking My Dream Boat*,' and, '*Someone to Watch Over Me*,' and, '*Stardust*,' and, '*Beer Barrel Polka*,' (got a lot of mileage from that one), and one of my favorites, '*Sonny Boy*,' (an Al Jolson song).

Some of the piano rolls even had words written on the scrolls so as the music played and the scroll progressed, so you could sing to the music. It was on that piano down there that I practiced how major and minor chords were made, and in the process, I learned some chord progressions.

And even when it was freezing cold in that already dank cement basement, I would play the piano and sing to my very basic tunes that I created. It was there that I composed the beginnings of "Old friend."

After we moved back to Glendora California, I lost touch and experience with playing with a piano and it wasn't until 1968 that actually had an opportunity to bring this song and the ideas of this song to the new level. The ideas of the lyrics in this song stem from the fact that I moved around so much that I lacked a reference point to deal with all the passing people along the way. Moreover, every time I moved, I had to leave everything behind; my toys, my clothes all possessions, and my friends. And letters did get harder to write as answers were few and many times came after I had moved to another location. But the sweet memories of that foot-petal player piano still return now and then, just like an "Old Friend."

After we moved back to Glendora California, I lost touch and experience with playing with a piano and it wasn't until 1968 that actually had an opportunity to bring this song and the ideas of this song to the new level. The ideas of the lyrics in this song stem from the fact that I moved around so much that I lacked a reference point to deal with all the passing people along the way. Moreover, every time I moved, I had to leave everything behind; my toys, my clothes all possessions, and my friends. And letters did get harder to write as answers were few and many times came after I had moved to another location. But the sweet memories of that foot-petal player piano still return now and then, just like an "Old Friend."

Side Note:

There is a jump out from this song a bit where I got forceful with my approach and attack on certain stanzas got me in trouble,...

Imagine this, it's 1970, we're up in the Catskills, (*we* meaning, my brothers John, Richie, Charlie and later, David, all in a twin bungalow that we rented for the summer for a thousand dollars) working hotels as waiters and working seasonal times, like Passover. I somehow managed to get Richie and Charlie hired on to work within Schenk's Hotel's dining room,...

Richie somehow passed by me and became head waiter with tables that looked out the windows and I got to have Charlie as my busboy. (and considering the fact that he was supposed to be 18 but was in reality, only 15, he caught on really quickly and all the old folks we had at out tables loved him and forgave him for his slowness in the beginning),...

Schenk's Hotel

Anyway I went to a party over at someone's place, one of the other waiters I believe, someone I don't think I knew, even then, but I got there and we got to talking and he asked me to play a song. I wasn't so good but I took him up on his offer. His piano was an older stand up box type.

So, I played this song on his piano and you remember that there's a jump out in this song,... where I get forceful with my approach and attack,... Well, fast forward couple weeks later a friend of this guy comes up to me and tells me I owe this other guy $250.00 to get his piano fixed. I told him it sounded just fine the last time I played it. I never heard anymore about this but since that time when I get to the part where there's a jump out and I get forceful with my approach and attack, I always take it a little easier.

It's Not Hard

(1991) –Oh, take it from me, it certainly is not hard to be callous, to be cold, to be disconcerted and have little or no empathy for others around you, especially if you've been wronged by them, it's so much easier to hold a grudge, to foster your own self-centeredness. And it is hard to forgive, it is not to not give up, and it's not hard to let go of a bad situation that you might have caused when the going gets tough.

And it's especially hard when you have to do this forgiveness alone;

exposing your vulnerabilities or weaknesses, and being proud and being big-headed only puts up more obstacles to get over, to get back where you used to be. In the end, I think it's part of the plan for our growth here on this earth; things we need to experience, adversity we need to endure through, and wisdom to be learned from mistakes so we might be able to rise above it.

She Wants To Fly

(1991) – There have been times that I have seen a certain look in Diane's eyes that hints of a desire for something else, somewhere else. I think of the life that I have provided for her and I have to know that sometimes it's not enough; sometimes I can just feel the energy in the room that whispers she would like something else, something that, most of the time, I cannot give her.

Diane with one of her many little friends

Sometimes just sitting at night watching the television just doesn't do it for her. And I know her life is busy with things she needs to do, or things she has to do, or things she feels if she doesn't do it would make her less of a person or wife so she does them; I know she's burdened with the need to take care of others and love them, and be the first with her hand up in the air to volunteer to give comfort and aid to the less fortunate or the sick or the elderly, or the charity to help the homeless, or to make her wonderful bread to share. She has a strong hope for a good tomorrow, and is standing in the light. And all this while she smiles back as if to say, it's okay, I'm fine. But sometimes; when she's not looking, I glance over at her and I see a different person; in her eyes

I see that she's thinking just what can be done so that we, as a couple, can stay close and not lose that magic that we have, or I see her gazing off into the distance, like an adventure is calling out to her, and she looks up to see an airplane passing over. And as she gazes up at that airplane going where ever it is going, it's like she's thinking things over; and that look on her face, that longing expression as she looks up to the skies as if to say, I wonder what it would be like to be able to fly.

Worried

(1991) – Worrying about necessary things as well as concerns that I shouldn't. This was another rendition of the song, "Worry" from the, "Something Must Be Wrong" album, but I was hoping to create a new feel for this tune. As I stated before, I was thinking about all the things I was worried about and sat down and documented this huge list ranging from personal health to political affairs. I was truly amazed at all the junk in my head that was slowing me down or affecting my karma. I'm not sure I accomplished what I hoped to, doing this over, even though this does sound different from the original two years earlier.

Side Note:

There is no way that I can get away from worry. There are many issues that come to mind, family, church, temporal things, physical things and dumb things that, according to their trivial or inadequate nature, have no right to haunt me—but they're there, sometimes commingling with other problems, all sharing my cognizant as well as my unconscious attention. And like an idiot I do give them voice and share in their concerns. Maybe everyone does this—I hope so.

Calm Down (All This Heat)

(1993) – As mentioned prior, this piece was one intended for words. It uses my In-Home Jazz and playing with sounds, their timbre and sustain, sometimes they come out weird too, and frankly, I never got past the first two words on either stanza. The first stanza has this,

"Calm down da da da, calm down da da da da da." And the second stanza, "All this heat, da da da da," And I just didn't find where I was going with either motif; the words weren't happening,... and so I was putting this away, but I thought it kind a made it without the need for lyrics,... and I'm glad I did,... years later I couldn't find the tape that had the recording,... and I been keeping a database record of my material from day one,... I am, after all, also a computer guy,... but this song in this recording session did not appear,... it was like,... well none the less, happy I recorded it after all,...

Windsor Chair

(1991) – The loss of physical buildings and chattel can be a sad thing, but the loss of a town's history, novelty and spirit, well that's a different thing, that can be a terrible loss. One night I was watching the news and saw this short article about a New England town in the town of Prescott Massachusetts that, because residents of their State needed water, Prescott became an underwater ghost town. Every-one was moved out to parts unknown leaving only certain residents that refused to abandon the area as their homes and livelihood were engulfed by the newly created Quabbin Reservoir.

I felt moved with the recorded interviews of some of the residents that had lived there and as they spoke with their New England ac-cents, they commented about the great loss of Prescott as well as the towns of Dana, Enfield and Green-wich which were all submerged in 1938.

Side Note: Arguably, this song did not achieve the effect I was trying to accomplish. The words were trite and the music did not move me like I had hoped it would.

From Far Away

(1993) – When I listen to this instrumentation, I see myself looking over to a far-seeing, deep-seated mighty, formidable set of trees in the mystical, magical, super-natural forest that will never be conquered, and will always stand tall.

To keep this vision alive, we must first figure out what is feasible, not being overly idealistic, and lean towards developing a conservation approach built on the principle of sustainable use and development of our rainforests and other forestation.

Beyond the responsible development of rainforests, efforts to rehabilitate and restore degraded forest lands along with the establishment of protected areas are key to securing rainforests for the long-term benefits they can provide mankind. We need to teach our children and others about the importance of our environment and how they can help save rainforests, and to restore the damaged ecosystems by planting more trees, many more trees on land where forests have been cut down, especially where clearcutting has raped the mountainsides. Just like when you want a sponsor to stop supporting that station, for a deceitful or immoral television personality we do need to bare down our support to and for those good companies that operate in ways that minimize damage to the environment. It would seem that it would be almost impossible to make these changes but it starts with urging people to live in a way that doesn't hurt the environment and continue to establish protected parks to safeguard the rainforests and wildlife.

97

- 29 - DREAMS FOR YOU
- 1994 -

98

※

NOTES ABOUT THE COVERS

Notes On The New Cover:

There's a lot to take in on this new cover; it too is a trip. First off, I created these rainbow spheres that encompass the borders, then there's the bolts of coloured lightnings in the background, then there's the dreamcatcher hovering in front of the lightnings, and this cover too has pictures in the picture when you stare deeply at it, and it has a lot of hidden images to be discovered, like, in a tiny portrait of Lord Baldwin himself nestled between the lettering, Dreams" and "For" Have fun.

Notes On The Original Covers:

The front cover, obviously another Buzby Berkeley scene from,... well, not sure anymore,... I went back and watched, '*42nd Street*' and, 'Dames' and all of the, '*Gold-digger*' movies but I could not find it,... but this picture? Really cool, right?

And the Back Cover;

"Afternoon on the Island of La Grande Jatte" by Georges Seurat, I just felt this painting was seated in fantasy or dream-like material.

99

〰

DREAMS FOR YOU

Dreams For You
Oh, In The Morning
In Passing
Meridith Anne
What Am I Doing With My Life?
Midnight River
Run With It
All Of This
For The Balance Of My Life

"Dreams For You," Copyright © May, 1994,
All Rights Reserved

100

Dreams For You

I'm lacking in much, and far from my ends,
I'll never measure up to expectations of friends.
I have my own theories; I won't play their role;
I believe in potential and the good of the whole.

But from all indications I'm close to my reach,
for you're here with me and we live happily.
I think of the things that we've gained from each day,
and though we're not there, we're sure on our way.

I have dreams; dreams to share.
They might come true, someday, somewhere.
I can't give you something I don't have to use,
but I've got enough of these dreams for you.

I can promise the moon and all those expensive toys,
but I'll never be in tight with the big money boys.
I have my own ways; I take things day by day,
and all these hopes I carry will not fade away.

From all the signs, I'm as rich as a king,
for you're here in my life; I have most everything.
You believe in me and it strengthens my life.
We share hopes for the future and the present's just fine.

But I have dreams for you, dreams to share,
they might come true, someday and somewhere.
I can't give you something I don't have myself to use,
but I've got more than enough of these dreams for you.

I have dreams for you Babe, dreams to share,
they might come true, someday, somewhere.
I can't give you something I don't have here to use,
but I've got more than enough of these dreams for you.

101

Oh, In The Morning

Sunshine is rising
over the hedges;
I think in the new morn
so clearly it seems.
Corn in the garden;
the dog's with the kids,
love in the household
all painted with dreams.
Oh, in the morning,
to wake a new soul,
while eating my breakfast
I plot out my goal.
And after the chores
we gather along;
each bringing their own,
we sing our new songs.
Oh, in the morning,...

102

In Passing

A glance, quick kiss and a wave heading out to our separate ways
all we have time for nowadays; in passing.
We wait outside of the door
looking back to reach once more,
as we question what it was all for; in passing.
The dispassionate, undeviating course
and pursuits structured to the source;
a thought of loss brings on remorse; in passing.
If we've learned anything from the past
we know our time here on earth goes fast,
and the aims, goals, the meanings, so vast; in passing.
The promise in good faith to weave
all the hopes; distant to believe,
for those dreams we strive to achieve; in passing.
In the end, we come in touch
with the questions we've asked so much
and the answers return with love; in passing.
A glance, quick kiss and a wave, heading out to separate ways
all we have time for nowadays; in passing.

103

Meridith Anne

Before the day begins; before the sun is set free,
she's already engaged in events soon to be.
One step ahead, from multiple fronts;
she knows where she's going; knows what she wants.
A laugh that delivers her wonderful smile,
will affirm you know you're in heaven for a while;
Meridith; Meridith Anne.

Determined and firm, decidedly head-strong;
she is ready to oppose the resistance and wrong.
Her ideas and convictions may portray a slight role,
but there's never a doubt who is in utmost control.
A look from her eyes confirms her resolve,
and tells you she knows who and what to involve;
Meridith Anne; Meridith Anne,

Meridith Anne, Meridith Anne,
knows where she's going; knows what she stands for, and,
a laugh that delivers her wonderful smile;
oh, Meridith; Meridith Anne.

Before the day ends, she's still on the run,
as she reviews her day and all that was done.
Ruling her affairs with compassion and care,
she shines on brightly to everyone there.
As fingers play on the black and ivory keys;
she sings clear and resonant, as easy as you please;
Meridith; Meridith Anne. Oh, Meridith; Meridith Anne.

104

What Am I Doing With My Life?

Here, I am just sitting on this couch;
thumbing through the want adds in doubt.
Thinking of some easier way out;
like I don't know what it's all about.
Goals and dreams of high school fade;
leave me to lose the plans I've made.
I know I've never made the grade,
and how can I know the game if I've never played?

What am I doing with my life?
What have I done with all my time?
Too late to go back and change the wrongs to right;
what am I doing; what am I doing with my life, with my life?

Looking back at what should or might have been;
it always comes to haunt me again.
I took the easy path to then, now my reward is what I am.
They say to stay in school or fall;

I should have listened to them all.
I'm running fast but I'm in a stall,
with my back here, against the wall.

What am I doing with my life?
What have I done with all my time?
Too late to go back and change the wrongs to right,
what am I doing; what am I doing with my life?

What am I doing with my life?
What have I done with all this time?
Too late to go back and change the wrongs to right.
What am I doing, what am I doing,...
with my life; with my life?

105

Midnight River

I was losing my mind and seeing life blind;
for a moment.
I was losing my dreams, coming apart at the seams;
for a moment.
I was hoping and praying to see you.
I was lonely and I dreamed that I could know you.
And feeling a vibration when you come near.
Good things about you is all that I hear,
and I know you could be kind;
you're like a midnight river in my mind.
I looked up at the Lord, "What can I afford?"
I asked him.
"All this loneliness I fight and I'm not sure if it's right."
I told him.
And a smile I see is from heaven.
As your eyes, I see are in heaven.
I almost feel the harmony it seems,
but it's lost somewhere; amongst all my dreams,
and what will I find,
in that midnight river in my mind.

106

Run With It

It's nobody's fault, there's no one to blame.
It just fell in your yard; now it's your game.
And there's no getting around it; there's no time to wait.
The time to act is now before it's too late.

And it's nobody's fault so don't go away;
you're in the groove, it's time to move,
run with it; hey, run with it, all the way.

This can't be avoided, now it's too late.
And your options are so few, consequences are so great.
Right now, it's hard to think
cause you're standing out of the light.
You need to do what's best, and what you know is right.

The actions are needed; anyhow, anyway.
You're the only one that'll get this done,
hey, run with it, mm, run with it, all the way.
Run with it. Oh, run with it, all the way.

107

All Of This

More than all those things you do
that keep the household pulling through;
the house, the clothes, the dishes, rugs and floors.
More than keeping up with kids, the little, medium and the big.

It's all of this; but there's more.

More than just the daily load that must be done to make life go,
to progress through the secret household war.
More than goals set on the run and rewards when the job is done,

and it's all of this; but there's more.
Yeah, there's all of this, it's all of this; but there's more.

So little passion left to sense. So little part of relevance.
So little time spent sharing all in store.
More than duty, girl or boy, you are important and need joy.

It's all of this, all of this; but there's more.
More than just the way you are when we get close or drift apart,

as needs and wants reduce to metaphors.
More than an attitudes or slip that make up a relationship,

well it's all of this, but it's more.
and it's all of this. Hey, it's all of this; but it's more.

And there's so much more to life, still we let it all slip by
till we look back when it's gone, and to what it was that we've done.

Gone away and gone away for good,
and our time leaves us here.

More than all the heart that burns;
the gentle touch
and true concerns
for everyone in your loving store.
More than all we share that's known,
the soft influence in this home,

well, it's all of this; but there's more.
And it's all of this. All of this; but there's more.
Yeah, there's all of this, you know
it's all of this; but there's more.

108

For The Balance Of My Life

Reach out, reach out, reach for what I would receive,
reach for what I truly believe;
can come true, and it will come true.

Give out, give out, give out as much as I can.
Give out and empty my hands
to those around, to those un-found.

One chance, one chance is all we're given to be found.
We've only one time around
to find the truth, to see and do,
and then it's through.

I need to do something special,
for the balance of my life.

So, teach; so teach, teach what I always wanted to learn.
Teach and set the passions to burn
in the heart, and every part.

Reach in, reach in, reach in to bring out what I could know.
Reach in and touch the very soul,
stir the fire; awake desires.

The time, the time runs short as we drift out of range.
We can't wait for differences to change
or go away, so I will stay; take hold today,

and do something special
for the balance of my life.

Reach out, reach out, reach for all that waits for your lead,
reach to meet the singular needs;
they're always there for one who cares.

Decide, decide, decide what I'm needing to do;
decide and then carry things through;
all I can be, for the symmetry of everything in me.

This life, this life; hard to see the forest from the trees
is filled with constant opportunities,
a unique wealth; as I lose myself for someone else.

Do something special
for the balance of my life.

Do something special
for the balance of my life.

109

MEMOIRS & NOTES - 29 -

Dreams For You

(1985) – After so much time I felt like it was time to write another love song for Diane. I like to be inspired, you know, have this wonderful tune come to me--or some inspirational words that might dictate the moment. But sometimes I just try to force something out; this was one of those. I was preoccupied with worrying about the holes in our lives, the unattended needs and deficits in life that cry out to be fulfilled and then the needs multiply and spill down to everyone else in the family. The more they go without, the more I feel inadequate in my career choices or that I have failed them in my task to support their needs, and it takes days to overcome this stupid misconception. The song is kind of leaning in that direction, apologizing for inadequacies but it has love to justify everything else.

Side Note:

Sometimes rushed songs have a contrived feel and lack that *special* magic that makes me feel good inside and reassures me that it, the song, has substance and value. And this composition started out that way,

Diane & I, about the time this song was written - 1985

but in my pursuit to put the music to the words, something happened and the chorus, which was the hook, came to own a life of its own, and in the end, rescued what could have been mediocre to its own greatness. So great in fact that it became the lead song and captured the name of the album. Days later I was singing the song in my head and realized that something was missing. I came back and added harmonicas and that bottom filling brass sound that you hear in the background. And although the varied sounds on the tape and the possible sounds that were voiced in my head were decidedly different, and still not quite what I wanted, I only had four tracks to work with and all four tracks were in use, so I polished some of the tracks, engineered the mix down, and then called it good; and this is what the results were.

Oh In The Morning

(1978) – The poem to this song was written at a time when I had three children, Lori, Chester III, and Elizabeth, and my life was a lot less complicated, perhaps because it was from some distant time ago when we were all less preoccupied with multi-media,

TV, computers, the internet and self-indulgent pursuits, we might have taken the time to take stock in our true blessings, like our interactions with our family and loved ones, and such. To me, this little poem had heart and such a good feeling that I shared the poem with both my mother and my father; hand wrote the poem on the side panels of a group of five photos of the family; Diane, Lori, Chet and myself, that were arranged and framed and then I sent them out as Christmas presents in 1978. I don't know what happened to the one that had I sent to my mother, but when my dad passed away in the fall of 2007, I retrieved the framed picture off the wall in the living room of the farmhouse where it had hung for 29 years. And it now hangs on our wall in our living room.

I think the choice of these particular photos in the frame managed to capture the friendly ambiance of our young, growing family (of five, at that time in 1978), as well as connecting itself with the, oh so warm-hearted feel of the poem. They went together so very well.

Side Note:

My Yamaha PRS-500 keyboard was not off limits to anyone, but there were rules; no pounding on the keys, no playing it without head-phones, no playing with it when they had their friends over,... I just wanted them to use it as a tool and not just a toy. And for the most part, the kids complied. Actually, I don't know much about who used it or when, except for Elizabeth. Liz was fascinated by the many voices as well as all the features that came with the keyboard.

One day in early 1993, I came home from work to find Liz (I think she was 15 at the time), playing with the keyboard. I was listening to the tune she was creating when she looked over and saw me standing there and smiled. She started the piece over so I could hear what it sounded like. It was kind of like, "Heart and Soul" and a little bit of "chopsticks" mixed together. She then told me excitedly how she discovered that the settings for any of the canned, single-finger accompaniments, that had five orchestration buttons, well, she discovered that the settings were programmable. I did not comprehend what she was saying and she knew it. She demonstrated that the sound I was hearing, a flute-like voice could, with the push of a few buttons, be changed to be an oboe or an accordion, or whatever voice I wanted to have it be. Moreover, she showed me that I could control the volume and other intrinsic settings for each voice I was using. All this time that I had done my recordings using the Yamaha keyboard, for over a year and a half, and after recording more than 17 albums with this **Yamaha PRS-500 keyboard,**

I had been pushing forward at maximum speed; full tilt boogie, to continue my ongoing quest to record my material; I was so focused on the end product that I never considered all the other possibilities this keyboard offered. Suddenly I had a greater capability to control the voices and give me a, "Wall Of Sound" and free up one or two of the limited four tracks available. It was an awesome find by Liz and I told her so on the spot. Moreover, I took those circular, independent tunes that were created by Elizabeth and embedded then into this here song. After I played around with it for a while, I then presented it to Liz, who said that she thought it sounded cool. And from those beginnings, I took the words of *"Oh in the Morning"* and created the rest of the music for this esoteric song.

This was the beginning of a new era for the Lord Baldwin material to follow that had lusher accompaniments and stronger resonances, all with more controlled volumes and tiny nuances to the reprogrammed voices; much of which nobody would know about unless they owned one of these keyboards and knew how to program them like I learned along the way in the next following 13 albums. It's funny to thing that if I had been hard-nosed and over-possessive with my musical instruments, this revelation would never have happened. And if you're reading this right now, thank you Liz; I really do appreciate all your scientific discoveries with the Yamaha PRS-500 keyboard. It totally changed my approach to my music.

In Passing

(1994) – Many of us are inundated with too much, too fast and everything we do seems to have this timeframe attached to it. So, everything should be measured to or on how much and how well things were accomplished within some finite timeframe. Just about the time I wanted to put this album together and most of the other work was already recorded and done, I had this kind of, inspiration. I was leaving for work, late, and I had barely finished glancing out the side window of the van as I waved goodbye to Diane, before I headed off to work, and the thought came to me that made me wonder, what kind of relationship is this, that all I have to offer my best friend, my wife and mother of all my nine, (soon to be ten) children, This person that I've spent most of my adult life with; all I have to give her is a three second glance and a wave of my hand? As you can read, I crammed a lot of stuff into this poem, and Diane thought I should simplify the words, especially in the third passage, but I did not; I did not want to lose the awesome feeling that I had experienced when I read this poem out loud right after I wrote it.

Meridith Anne

(1993) – I wish there was a way that I could capture the essence of the wonderfulness and eclectic personality of Meridith Anne, but that isn't possible and I was left with trite substitutions and tiny generalities that don't even scratch the surface to who and what Meridith Anne is all about. But I think I did capture a little bit of her energy, her tenacity, her enthusiasm and her heart in the words of this poem/song. And oh, then there's Meridith Anne who performs and dances and sings in her own way on whatever stage she is set upon. And how magnificent her performances and how wonderful her singing is.

The funny thing is, out of all of my children, she appears to have the most interest in my creative works, she has read most of my books, she has listened to many of my albums and is interested in all my works in progress, but I don't believe she has this album or even a copy of this song; but who has cassettes right now, and even if they do, who has a cassette player nowadays?

Side Note: Two weeks before Meridith was born, Diane was sure it was time and we went to St Peters hospital only to have them send us home again. Nearly a week later the same thing; Diane was sure it was time and they sent us back home again.

On the night she was born, in fact, as Diane and I were literally walking out the front door of our house, there stood my mother, who with her husband Ron had driven a camper-van all the way from New Jersey. She was smiling as she came in and I told her that it was really 'the time,' this time, and she said that she would hang out with the other three kids while we went to get Meridith delivered.

Another Side Note:

For three weeks prior, we had decided to name the new baby, Bonnie Jean. So, after the delivery I saw a name, "Meridith Anne" on the new-born hospital bassinette. When I went into see Diane, who told me this story; "after we got to the hospital, I heard a small voice in my head say, "My name is Meridith Anne."" As she was getting ready to be wheeled into the delivery room, she heard that voice again say, "My name is going to be Meridith Anne." And like one of the verses to the poem declares;

"Determined and firm, decidedly head-strong"

That has been the mantra and signature attribute that Meridith has exemplified and continues to follow her whole life. That attribute has helped her to go to Korea to teach, to go back to college and get two Masters degrees and to follow her heart.

What Am I Doing With My Life?

(1989) – My whole life was unraveling, the place I was working at, JW Electronics, was indeed going out of business and I had no other recourse or plans to do anything else. Oh, I had thought of a lot of things I could do, but all of them required training or education that I didn't have. In fact, I was family and so I wasn't just kind of hanging around there. Yes, there was a hope that that things might change and that I might possibly start making some big money, and that my father-in-law might just recognize my potential and that things financially would turn around for me and for JW Electronics. You know, there are an awful lot of wishes and hopes in all that stuff, but none of those wishes ever came to pass and although I was kind of looking for other work, in the end, like it or not, I was a part of this family and I did not bail or leave there until the doors to the store finally closed.

Side Note: Chet and I were on a Boy Scout camp out at Squaxin Island, which is a little island outside of Olympia on Puget Sound owned by the Squaxin Indian tribe, and I was sitting on a rocky shore chucking stones into the water while taking stock of all of my options; trying to figure out just what I ought to do. And like many of us career-minded music folks do, I was evaluating and reevaluating my circumstances and was inspired to write this poem,...

Many of us consider the bar that we aspire to, as being so high that we end up getting discouraged in the process, and we lose sight of the real purpose of the journey. While I was playing mind games with myself about my talents, skills and capabilities, or the lack of them, it started to rain, and although all the boys were oblivious to it all, getting wet while they kept goofing around, I chose to go into my tent and try to remain dry. I pulled out a pencil and small pad from my pack and wrote the words to this poem during that downpour. About 20 minutes later, the rain stopped coming down, we all got back together again and played a game of baseball.

All the time I was out in left field or up at bat or just standing around, I was thinking about the words to the poem and thinking about what music I could put with those words.

Another Side Note:

Arguably, someone else, an outsider maybe,... might look at some of Lord Baldwin's material and try to reflect on what Lord Baldwin had accomplished and then that person might say something to the effect, "I don't see it. there's nothing special about this guy and nothing out of the ordinary about his writings or for that mater, his music." and I'm thinking that for them and their circumstances, they might just be right,... I may not be what they're looking for,... and in my journey I have crossed into a lot of genres and let's face it, Lord Baldwin is not for everyone,... and let's say, it's not for you,... that's okay,... nobody likes everything all the time,... but if you're someone that finds Lord Baldwin's material interesting? Well that becomes fuel for me to persist,... persevere,... reason to keep doing it,... reason to do more,... reason to continue doing what I'm doing,... giving me purpose and maybe an answer to, *"What Am I Doing With My Life?"*

Midnight River

(1973) – New love is like that fast-running river in the night that can neither be gauged of its activities nor easily slowed down from its purpose and destination. This particular poem was written for Diane a couple months prior to us getting married. If it sounds like I'm indecisive, confused, and yet uncommonly optimistic, that's probably because that was the way I was back then.

This was decidedly an instant hit with Diane and even some of her friends, so I played it a lot, and actually, I burned out on it and just kind of stopped playing it for quite some time. Still, I was doing gigs around Portland, coffee shops, Bars, gatherings and even radio stations; trying to get Lord Baldwin heard and noticed by the powers that be, but it was all to no avail. Anyway, this was one of the old standby songs that I would pull out to mellow things out after playing a fast song. This particular recording does not really do justice to what this song has sounded like when done in front of an audience where I'm fed by the enthusiastic crowds, and many of my interpretations in the past reflect a calmer, flowing sound. But this recording did capture the general feel of what I was trying to say and display with my music.

Side Note:

By the time I wrote this poem Diane was working for the telephone company making good money.

She moved out of the place with Sally and moved to the Ong-ford Apartments and into a tiny, one-room flat on the third-floor with a foldaway kitchen and a murphy bed. It was really cool. And in a way, not having any more negative digs and innuendos from Sally was a plus, but even though I knew I was improving all the

%The Ongford Apartment - Downtown
Portland

time, without the unconstructiveness and forced pessimism factor from Sally there was now no way to gauge whether or not Sally would be surprised that my music was sometimes impressive. Sally also had a new boyfriend that liked my music and songs but he also knew that Sally did not want him to give me the impression that I was anything but an untalented guy that would waste his life pursuing music, writing songs that would ultimately, never get him anywhere.

Run With It

(1992) This song advised myself to get over Chris's passing and stop blaming myself, and stop blaming other people, but instead look in-side and continue to reconstruct that thing that is the essence of me. I will always be his father and he will always be in my thoughts and prayers. Sometimes we have to deal with life's adversities in spite of our inadequacies but you know, sometimes it would be good to be able to pass that difficulty on to someone else or for the problem to go away, but in the end, our trials are for our own education and sometimes, our own personal growth. Hardships seem to be the defining moments of our lives where we lose everything and in return, we struggle to gain a better understanding of the special people still in our lives and the people around us; and maybe more importantly, a stronger understand-ing of ourselves. Of course, that's all easier said than to have to live through, but still, it did make me feel better to sing about it, to think about it, and to realize that it was time to move on, and run with it.

Side Note:

The essence of the music to this poem/song came to me; the music seemed to materialize out of the air and so quickly, and the words fit in to the musical slots so perfectly that I feel it was because I was inspired. It is a great song. And you know, it is because of songs like this one or "What Am I Doing With My Life?" that keeps me grounded but moving forward. I listen to the words and say, "Yeah, that's what I was trying to say" or when the marriage of music and word come together so well, my heart swells.

At the time I'm writing this there have not been any person, company or organization beating down my door looking for the mastermind that created all this stuff, and it's hard for me to imagine that it will ever happen in my lifetime, but the fact that you are reading this note right now, well it gives me a good feeling that someone out there found me, and moreover was interested enough to take my compositions seriously enough to read the poems and maybe even, listen to the songs that partner and coincide with the poetry.

Just know that, aside from the fortune and fame that was fleeting to begin with and I made my choices to follow the other paths that I did, being a family man, being a good husband and taking the time to be a good person; ultimately, all I ever truly wanted was some kind of validation that what I was doing all these years had value, and hopefully, my songs, my poetry, my music, made you feel good in the process. I was doing this thing for me, but I was also doing it for you.

All Of This

(1991) – My love, Diane, gets up early every day, does all her chores and motherly duties and continues until evening and then retires to bed. I'm sure that, at times, she gets weary of her simple lot in life, and it can be hard to see the differences that she makes in my life as well as so many other people's lives.

I have always had my music calling me, and my hopes were always to do something with all of this material sometime in the future. But while that never happens, Diane has immersed herself into the raising of our children and she continues to go forth to spread her charity and good works with those in need, and of course, she has to deal with a neurotic me, who has forever, not only appeared oblivious to all the work around the house that she's doing, but this loafer seems aloof, and at times distant, as he trails off to his little section of the bedroom to work on some new material.

And I saw her there; no one raising the banner and shouting accolades for her triumphs and successes, no one reinforcing an appreciation for all she was doing; I remember thinking that it would be hard to believe that Diane was not frustrated. So, I wrote this poem and song in hopes of cheering her up, and at the same time, recognizing her victories and accomplishments, and in this weird way, sending out my love to her. I just wanted her to know that, although I appeared to be ignorant of all the little things she did, I did know, and I did value her, and I was grateful for the woman, and I wanted her to know that all those little things that she does on a daily basis that nobody knows or seemingly nobody cares, well, she and her constant positive energy shores me up and gives me a certain strength to carry on,... and write my little songs; like this one.

Side Note:

At the time I'm writing this, Brian is now seven and in the first grade. Diane has been getting out of the home more and has recently finished volunteering for the 2000 Census. She has also been working in the genealogy library at the church and seems to know what she's doing; she's made new friends and I think it has made her happier.

For The Balance Of My Life

(1994) – Having a sense of purpose in life is very important to me. There are so many things that we have to balance in our lives—work, family, play, leisure, relaxation, caring for others, caring for ourselves, social consciousness, political consciousness, environmental consciousness, religious beliefs and activities, physical needs; things most of us are balancing, often without realizing it, all of the time. It is a recurring theme in much of my material and, if life continues on this same plane, will continue on. I know that balance is a state of mind and I'm not sure what that looks like. I am sure that balance doesn't look like "balance," and it seems that in my poetry and words, I preach on many levels and almost seem to have all the answers, but I, like you, I am struggling to get by, hoping I'm doing the right things, repenting my past sins and I'm hopeful for a good tomorrow. I am working on teaching Diane to say no. It is a critical piece in reducing stress and balancing her life, (and mine).

We all have a choice about how we live our lives; a choice of activities to be involved in and a choice of people to be around us. I try to avoid negativity,... but I have to know and accept that I just can't do everything all of the time.

Watching Diane managing herself echoes her sense of empowerment in what she can do in a day, and in a lifetime. I get this power of choice, and knowing what situations, happenings, things good or bad that I have control over, and I have to realize what I have no control over. But a life oriented around a passionate purpose is one that is much easier to keep in balance. It is in that balance of my life, that hope beyond the struggles of the everyday that I put my energies into.

Side Note:

In my Senior year, I was moved into my dad's house along with my brother Richie. We were kind of dumped off by my mother who was worried about Richie and me and thought maybe my dad could turn us round right,... There is a longer story to this that may get told another time, but for now,... Suddenly I had a father,... arguably after I was mostly grown,... and we found our dad to be pleased with our arrival, especially so as to have two new farm hands to do his chores for him,...

Richie and I grew to like doing the chores, although Richie had a hard time getting up at five thirty in the morning so I ended up being the designated cow milker and Richie would come out (much later) to throw hay at the horses and slop the pigs,... After we'd been there a while, we found that our dad was a good man and someone that cared about what we were up to,... and over time, there were a few good lessons and good skills that I learned and incorporated into my own fatherhood skills to be used for the balance of my life and incorporated into my own family skills.

Me & the Pop looking in his farmer-town newspaper

By the way, someone in my senior math class gave me her copy of, 'the Hobbit' and after getting a fedora from the Goodwill, I got the felt all wet and using a broom handle, I made that dwarf-hobbit hat that you see my dad wearing there. In fact, he liked it so much, he wore it around the farm and ultimately, he never gave it back.

110

- 30 - CITY BOY - 1994 -

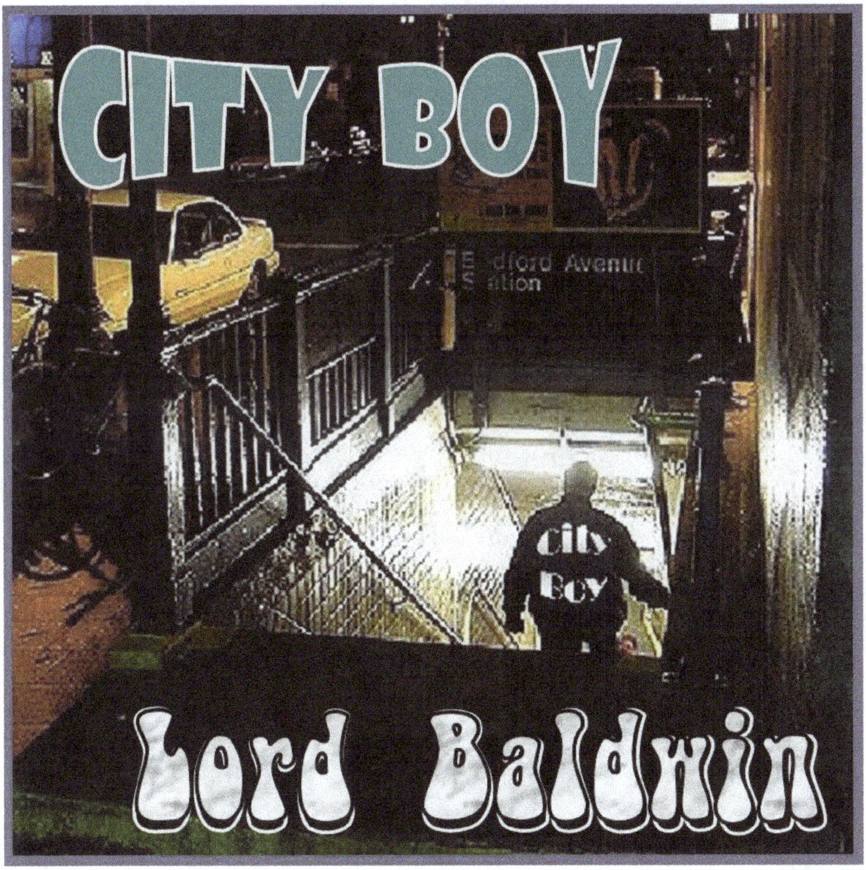

III

NOTES ABOUT THE COVERS

Notes On The New Cover:

The new cover, like the original back cover, but a bit enhanced, again reflecting the almost gritty feel of living in the city; Bedford Avenue Station Subway, Located at the intersection of Bedford Avenue and North Seventh Street in Williamsburg in Brooklyn; the feel of the cold permeating the darkness of night; the illuminated hole of the underground cave that our protagonist is cautiously braving, descending into; the ever present taxi cab, trolling for a fare; the bicycles chained to a lamppost, (which does not deter most thieves); it's all here on the cover.

Notes On The Original Covers:

The front original cover was from a postcard in the late 40s of New York City that I found down a rabbit hole of the internet. I was hoping that the lettering of my pseudonym would look like a blimp hovering over the city,... even now, I'm not sure that that worked out.

The original back cover reflected the feel of living in the city; Bedford Avenue Station Subway, night time, taxi cab, bicycle chained to a lamppost,... It was (and probably still is), a rapid transit system that is a part of the New York City Transit Authority, which is itself controlled by the Metropolitan Transportation Authority of New York.

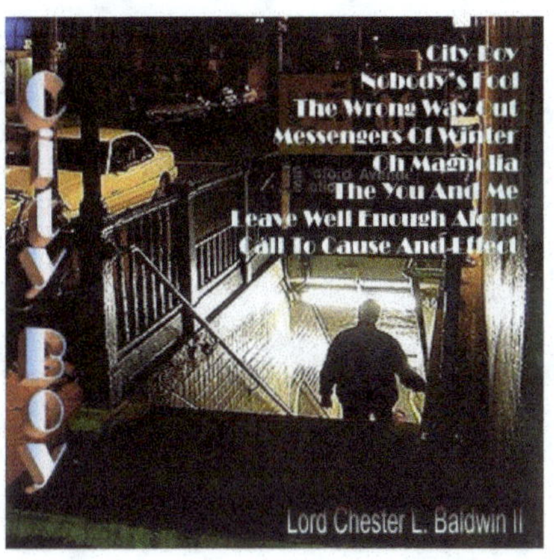

Side Note: For a small while in 1970, I lived in Brooklyn and not having a car, I used the New York City Subways. I traveled using the Bedford Avenue Station Subway, (exclusively 'the, 'L' line') which turned out to be my gateway to four of the five boroughs of New York City; *the Bronx, Brooklyn, Manhattan,* and *Queens.*

112

CITY BOY

City Boy
Nobody's Fool
The Wrong Way Out
Messengers Of Winter
Oh Magnolia
The You And Me
Leave Well Enough Alone
Call To Cause And Effect

113

City Boy

Sun coming up, with so much to be done.
See the little people down there, all on the run.
Another five minutes and I'll be one;
a city boy;
yeah, a city boy.

Concrete and steel runs in all directions for miles.
Like the Tower of Babel, buildings reach for the sky.
I know that I'm here but I can't say why
I'm a city boy;
yeah, a city boy.

People with an attitude, they're strained and uptight,
argumentative and hostile; always ready for the fight,
Pugnacious and polemic but I love this life
of a city boy;
yeah, of a city boy.

From the airway to the streets to the underground below,
people move in masses, hurry up, wait and go.
Just being can be a hassle in desolation row
for a city boy;
yeah, a city boy.

The day is never done, the metropolis never sleeps.
Nocturnal creatures, like roaches start to creep
to do the something always happening out here on the streets
for a city boy,
yeah, a city boy.

Night lights flicker as the wind-blown trash goes by.
Vampires and reprobates mete out the last-minute lie.
Still the all-night music down the avenue's sounding pretty fine
to a city boy,
yeah, a city boy.

Shadows shift and fade; the sun will be here soon.
With the dawn at my back, and my harmonica's lonesome tune
I head on down the sidewalk, I'm the king of all these ruins
the city boy,
yeah, the city boy.

Yeah, the city boy;
the city boy,...

114

Nobody's Fool

Always in control, no need to play some role.
I know just what I want, how to act and what to say.
I always follow through, no one tells me what to do,
I made my own success doing things my way.
Still as I manage and regulate, suppress and dominate,
it drives almost everyone else away.

I'm nobody's fool so I play things real cool,
still, it all seems so cruel at night when I'm alone.
I'm nobody's love, and when push comes to shove,
all the dreams I dream of, leave me here, on my own.

I rarely get asked out, but if I do, I try to route
them to some other distant avenue.
So scared to play along, that I might do something wrong,
I just dismiss them without further ado.
At times, on some nights; staring at the northern lights,
I wonder what it's like to follow through.

I'm nobody's fool so I play things real cool,
yet, it all seems so cruel at night when I'm alone.
I'm nobody's love, and when push comes to shove,
all the dreams I dream of, leave me here, on my own.

I'm in desperate need of love but I'm so afraid;
I don't know how to leave this life I've made,

I'm nobody's fool so I play things real cool,
still, it all seems so cruel at night when I'm alone.
I'm nobody's love, and when push comes to shove,
all the dreams I dream of, leave me here, on my own.

115

The Wrong Way Out

So much is missing in the translations,
the intentions clearly suspect.
Going too far or not enough;
questions of an abuse or neglect.

Claims and allegations, focused on designs ill planned,
only leave a sorted picture, that no one could understand.

In the end, the give and take without knowing what it's all about,
only justifies the frail and assailable
to pursue the wrong way out.

Tomorrow's almost here; today is here and gone,
the dreams of immortality are for those
that anticipate the dawn.

Reaching for the moon, with hands that grope about
The holocaust, raging within;
the anguish exposed without.

In the end, as we sit in judgment
without knowing what it's all about,
the disillusioned children descend to the wrong way out.

So much missing in the translations;
the intentions clearly suspect.
And it's going too far or not enough
with questions of abuse or neglect.

Claims and allegations, focused on designs ill planned,
only leave a sorted picture, that no one could ever understand.

In the end, the give and take
without knowing what it's all about,
only justifies the frail and assailable
to pursue the wrong way out.

116

Messengers Of Winter

Messengers of winter
came to me this morning,
painted in the sunrise.
Long necked ducks
flying over head,
and the clouds rolled in.
As I come to you, I wonder,
will we make it in our dawning?
Preludes of breaking sunshine;
out our window,
winter breezes bite to the bone;
and the clouds rolled in.
Messengers of winter
came to me this evening,
painted in the sunset.
White snow falling
in the cold, black night;
and the clouds rolled in.

117

Oh Magnolia

Oh, Magnolia,
oh, Magnolia. Oh, Magnolia.
Shinning like the sun through the trees,
blooming fragrant flowers with ease.
Magnolia.

Oh, Magnolia. Oh, Magnolia.
Floating like a cloud on a breeze,
living life the way that you please,
oh, please Magnolia,

I've got these frustration blues,
and I've come to the realization it's you.
You,... Magnolia.

Oh, Magnolia.
Oh, Magnolia.

Oh, Magnolia, oh, Magnolia.
Oh, Magnolia.

118

The You And Me

I've made mistakes; come away more than once with regret.
and I have learned to deal with life and take what I get,
but I've never crossed a chasm like this yet;
it separates the bond from free, it separates the You and Me.
The times gone by are treasures I hold now deep within.
The dreams we shared for so long in a way would just begin,
and everywhere I go from everywhere I've been;
within my heart I see all the pieces of the You and Me.
I grow weary of the voices that don't know.
I want to run away with nowhere left to go.
I feel a hope that dwindles with the night and so,
there's a comfort in the needs and the thoughts of the You and Me.
I've made mistakes; yeah,...
and I've come away more than once with regret.
and I've learned to deal with things in my life,
and I've learned to take just what I get,
but I have never crossed a chasm like this yet;
it separates the bond from free,
and it separates the You and Me.
The You and Me.

119

Leave Well Enough Alone

I'm foolish to believe she will ever need
the love we used to have before the end.
But I keep my hold, maybe just for hope,
she'll decide to change her mind again.

And I'm pondering what to do, and yet I know the truth,
she won't need me; she'll be fine on her own.
I only fooling myself; she needs someone else,
I should just leave well enough alone.

I still have my space, I'm not so out of place,
here with her, the kids and the couch.
Yet things ain't so great, we don't communicate,
and I think, "Why don't just I move out."

Although the love is gone, I keep holding on,
to change her will that's solid as a stone.
I'm here wasting time; they'll all be just fine,
and I should just leave well enough alone.

This heart burns and aches, still hoping for the change;
a change from the track that we're on.
but it falls through the cracks and comes down to facts,
that the fire, the passion is gone.

I'm foolish to believe that she will ever see
me as anyone but the guy she once knew.
Aside from fading away and hoping for some day,
there's not much else that I can do.

With no serious talk and the lines cut or blocked,
I'm only living in this neutral zone.
She doesn't need me at all, I'm just the guy down the hall,
and I should just leave well enough alone.

120

Call To Cause And Effect

It just burns me up, and it's gone too long,
how some people can think, there's nothing wrong.
To live the fool's paradise; ignoring the turn,
and taking without thought of any return.

The selfish rejoice in their quest for greed
and confusion rules over want and need.
To ignore or exploit or even deny
is to deceive the child and live in the lie.

Hey, it's all a call to cause and effect
when abuse is second only to neglect.
We cannot hide, no matter where we run,
if we don't act now, tomorrow may not come.

Runs from bad to worse with an impending doom,
as we watch it all happen in our private living room.
We see mass starvation; people living in fear,
but it seems so distant like, it can't be happening here.

As the earth is ravaged, we get more out of touch,
as we're told by the careless that it won't matter much.
Put on plastic facades that hang on great walls
while taking without giving and destroying us all.

It's all just a call, to cause and effect,
when abuse is second only to neglect.
It's too late to hide and it's too late to run,
if we don't act now, tomorrow may not come.

Do we care about our lives, or are we so naïve,
do we care about children and the world that we leave?
To realize an urgency from all it will allow,
because if we really care, it's time to care now.

Hey, it's all a call to cause and effect
when abuse is second only to neglect.
It's too late to hide and too late to run,
if we don't act now, tomorrow may not come.

MEMOIRS & NOTES - 30 - 'CITY BOY'

City Boy

(1994) - There was some time early in the summer of 1970 where the Concord Hotel in upstate New York was doing a lockout to prevent the union from getting their demands. My brother David was a union organizer, and at the forefront of the whole movement, but like me and many other waiters and busboys, we were all in between jobs for a couple of weeks.

I was with my friend Michael, who was a heroine addict that was trying to kick the stuff. I was trying to help him, but I had no idea what he was going through or what I could do to help him. We were down to the city, kind of looking for work, but having

The Concord Hotel's Main Dining Room - 1970

a good time along the way. We stayed in the Bronx for a while, then we were in Queens for short time, we stayed in Brooklyn right by Prospect

Park for a while, but nothing seemed to come around as far as work was concerned.

One day we decided to give it one more chance and we headed for . About 8:00 at night it started getting cold and we decided we probably would need a room. We stopped at this place, I'm not sure how to describe this place without saying flophouse, but after we paid our money and went up to the room, we both felt a little uneasy about that place. Maybe it was the smell, a kind of small, faint smell of rotting garbage, or maybe it was the rundown hallways and holes in the door, or maybe it was the company around us, the rot-gut winos or down and out bums that flanked the doorways and halls as we walked to our room, and maybe it was a combination of all of this, but the price was right so we went into our room. We were not there more than five minutes before the cockroaches seemed to bleed out of the walls and they were everywhere. Michael and I were no strangers to cockroaches or that type of environment, but he looked over at me and I looked back at him and without any words we picked up our stuff and went back down to the front desk.

Greenwich Village in the late 60s - early 70s

The desk clerk on seeing us coming down so soon, asked, "What's wrong?" Michael and I looked at each other, and then I told the clerk that we wanted our money back because the room was full of cockroaches. The clerk denied that his facility had any problems, but at the same time asked us to keep our voice down. I told the clerk that I would be glad to go upstairs and fill my shoe with the roaches I could pull off the wall. The clerk then angrily mumbled something under his breath, opened up the cash register, and handed us back our money. He made some insinuation that we went up into the room just to have some place to shoot our drugs.

At first, we thought we'd pull an all-nighter just drifting from head shop to head shop, listening to the underground music, getting lost in the psychedelic posters, interacting with the night people that like vampires never see the light of day. We grabbed a couple of slices of pizza at 1:30 in the morning, and generally just hung out with all the other hippies; and there were a lot of people out on the streets. This roaming around lasted until about 4 o'clock in the morning, when it got real cold and, because of the different building configurations, the wind was blowing in different directions seemingly at the same time. We decided to take another plan and hopped on one of the subways that eventually headed back into Manhattan. One train led to another until about 6:30 in the morning where we emerged out from the IRT Broadway–Seventh Avenue Line, onto the Wall Street Station. And there we were, at the intersection of Wall Street and William Street in the Financial District of Manhattan.

As we walked down that deserted street, I pulled out my Hohner Marine Band harmonica from my pocket and started playing the blues. The morning sun was warming my back and I kind of felt that I had defeated the night monster and at that moment I was now the king, surveying all my domain of all those skyscrapers and buildings around me, and at that moment; so I was.

Nobody's Fool

(1993) - Sometimes you find control has a double edge sword and as you may be confused or annoyed by others' inadequacies and their reactions, life is not what you hoped it might be. I recorded this piece a little while earlier and it would have gone on one of my earlier albums but I ran out of time and room, so this new album became a perfect place for this song to exist.

Side Note:

There was this guy working at JW Electronics that was less than civil to anyone else, especially anyone he felt was below him, and because his value system was centered around money, anyone that made less money than him was maybe considered less intelligence, certainly a subordinate and lesser or altogether inferior to him. Mr. Arrogant also felt that he was God's gift to all women, and he treated them like that. I'm sure there were some girls that liked how he would flash around money, driving around in his custom British-racing-green,1968 Dodge Charger with the 330 horsepower, four-barrel, 383-V-8 engine, and he could be seen with someone new every week or so. I heard that he was even married for a time, and it is my hope that he still is and has a family; I hope that he is not somewhere out there, alone with nothing but his money to keep him company.

Another Side Note:

Clichés can be wonderful beginnings for songs, especially when the hook takes on a double meaning. I took this scenario of being nobody's fool and modeled the protagonist to be a sharp, intelligent, independent, wealthy but perhaps even calculating person, that, deep down, like all of us, was just another lonely person in need of acceptance and love.

The Wrong Way Out

(1992) - Life can be so confusing when you go through it without any instructions or a road map. Are we all not, in some way or another, lost and confused and perhaps even going the wrong direction? And if we choose to continue, for whatever reason, in that wrong direction, does it then become the right way, and if so, when does that happen? Then there's the problematic circumstances that dictate the philosophies that mandate the person's actions. If you're not part of that running solution, are you really part of the problem or just an annoyance in someone's breakfast conversation?

And then there's teenagers. And what we say is not always interpreted to what it is that we meant. Maybe part of the message is received but sometimes important parts of the instructions are misconstrued and then mistakes are made, things happen, and who knows what consequences befall the victims in the wake.

And it's not always their fault. Misunderstandings lead to misjudgments or miscalculations that can end in disaster, yet from what their understanding of the task or the recommendation or instructions that were given, they did what they were told, working with the limited tools they had to work with.

With all the erroneous information out there declaring its truthfulness, and the tilted directions that we are pointed towards, and the invalid results that we want but can never achieve, if we look beyond moral considerations, through or even past political contemplations, (hard to do, too hard), who or what ultimately should be able to make the final decisions that some action or direction will be the right one and what happens when we learn we went the wrong way after all?

Politically we have been boycotting Cuba for thirty years, because of Castro, but many businesses have argued that trading freely with Cuba would be good for Cuba and the United States. I'm aware of the fear that some of the Republicans have with the 

Cuban-American people and their voting power, but has the embargo and the boycotting of Cuba really accomplished anything but bringing our relations with them and others around the world to a standstill?

In the end, the give and take without knowing what it's all about, only justifies the frail and assailable to pursue the wrong way out.

Messengers Of Winter

(1973) - There comes a time when a person makes a decision to do something or go somewhere because he or she feels that it is the right thing to do, in spite of the fact that it may be the hardest thing they have ever done. This song materialized after one of my friends, who married early, took his wife and moved to some place in the wilderness of Alaska. This is the early '70s and people were trying to hold on to the ideals and concepts of a kind of united order, living as a hippie in a commune to escape the problems and trappings and unrighteous dominions of the real world they faced.

Unfortunately, here in the lower 48 states, this type of lifestyle was rapidly dissolving, especially in the right-wing states of the south that included hippies in their suffocated civil rights agendas. As times changed, there were some hidden pockets in Colorado, Oregon, Washington State and in Northern California, but many of the communal regimes were deteriorating with ambiguous purposes, indefinable philosophies, imprecise directions for the future with dwindling numbers, and nobody wanted to say, "it's over."

But there was still the unlimited potential of the frontier of Alaska, and so my friend Bob and his wife Jan loaded up their cream-coloured, 1963 Ford Falcon station wagon, and drove away, never to be seen or heard from, by any of us, again.

Side Note:

I thought to myself, what kind of bold, brash, attitude would I have had to have if I would have wanted to go with Diane and try to make this move? And what kind of adjustments, compromises, sacrifices would we need to endure to make this happen? So this song turned out to be a kind of questionable observation as Bob and Jan arrived in late summer to set up house in an environment they knew nothing about, but with a positive hope for the future, they prepared to face the onset of winter.

Another Side Note:

This was maybe the one pivotal song that distinguished me and my talents to be something more than just a guy with a guitar and a dream. One day I called Diane up and told her I had a new song and that I was excited to share it with her. She suggested that I come over for a home-cooked meal and then play the song for her afterwards. It was a Friday night, I arrived at the apartment Diane shared with two other girls. I had been there a couple times before and I knew I was not well received, partially because I had, (maybe still have?) a brash personality that especially grated on some girls, and partially because her roommates saw me as a threat to take away the wonderful person that volunteered to do their laundry, their free housekeeping and their dish washer.

Dinner was great, and we all settled into the living room area. Pulling out my guitar, I played a couple songs. Then I pulled out the folded paper that had the words to this poem and played, 'Messengers Of Winter.' When I finished, Diane said that she really liked the song, but Sally, who I expected was going to comment on the second refrain where I missed a beat and had to play catch up, looked dumbfounded. I mean it was like she had come to the realization that there was hope for me after all. And it was a pivotal moment for me as I realized my most nitpicking, unsympathetic, fault-finding critic was impressed by my work. At that moment she could have said anything negative but I wouldn't have believed it. To this day I am grateful for the Sally that I experienced that evening. There was a great weight of uncertainty lifted from my shoulders and I knew I had something special in my poetry and my music. It was one thing to have others obligatorily complement me in passing after I had played a song or two, but it was truly something else to suddenly know that I was good; that I could, in earnest, believe in myself.

Oh Magnolia

(1974) - Beauty can be found in the most unusual places. Here again is one of my old standby songs that I played to death, but somehow it never seemed to lose its good feeling.

I saw a picture of a flowering Magnolia plant in a magazine and its beauty impressed me. I combined that beauty with the personality of this person I knew back in 1973 and thus his song was created. And who is Magnolia? I think you may all know.

The You And Me

(1994) – Reflecting on a time gone by and the pain of loss can consume a person to disillusionment. I've had people tell me that I ought to get over this grieving process and get on with my life. When I worked at the Forest Funeral Home I was required to take some classed to get myself ready to be a Funeral Director. One set of classes was called, "Life Appreciation" where I learned that, until you experience an unfortunate, terrible loss you should not ever say, I know how you feel, because you don't. Everybody's circumstances are different, but even if you have experienced a great loss, you still cannot tell someone that you know how they're feeling. Everybody's grieving process is different. So for someone to tell me that I need to get over it; well, they mean well.

Christopher's passing stayed with me, it haunted me, returning like an unknown shadow that toys with me as it crosses over or waits on the outside of my peripheral vision, preventing me from getting a clear look, and as I turn quickly to see who or what the shadow is, I'm left with nothing.

And all those people telling me to get over this—who are they? How can they tell me they know how I feel if they've never gone through this process before, and even if they have gone through this process, how can they know of the love that I would have for my son, by gauging the type of love they have?

And as he marches back into my life, softly calling out to me and then passing by like the wind through the trees, I accept my pain and solemn calling because, like a marriage for better or worse, in sickness and health, so he is to me, one of my sons, in life and in death.

Side Note:

I have always felt that, besides the music stemmed into my very soul, one of the greatest talents that God has endowed to me is this oversensitive heart that aches too easily and is broken too often. (Meridith also has this curse-blessing; such an awesome, sensitive spirit). But that gift also includes a way to document the pain and sorrow in the words of my poetry and the music in my heart, and I'm so very thankful for that wonderful gift.

> *"I've made mistakes, come away more than once with regret.*
> *I've learned to deal with things in my life,*
> *and to take just whatever I get;*
> *but I've never crossed a chasm like this yet;*
> *it separates the bond from free,*
> *and it separates the You and Me."*

Another Side Note:

As you have been reading, you may have surmised that my childhood was not so charming, but in truth, I knew nothing else so for me it was normal.

My biggest bright side was going through all that stuff with my brother Richie who, most of the time, revered me and my big-brother leadership.

A story came from our past as we were up in Anchorage Alaska after Senior got a job with Standard Oil to run a service station there,... Meanwhile, Grandpa Scarbrough, drove 2,800 mi, (in 5 days) via the Alaskan Highway, to go fishing, When

he arrived, he bought Richie and I new red boots and he had gotten Richie and I, new raincoats with matching fisherman's rain hats; Richie with a red coat and hat and me with a yellow coat and hat. We were pretty jazzed by them and had a hard time taking them off, even for bedtime.

One morning, after a long rainy night, we headed out with no place in particular, and after crossing the railroad tracks, we decided to head down to the water. The tide was out and there was a huge dark gray mudflat that stretched out to the water and down the coastline for miles. Feeling invincible with our new rain gear, we pressed forward, determined to go to the water's edge.

When we got closer to the water, the mud became increasingly deeper until the gray mud came up to the middle of our boots. It was a weird mud, not sand but not dirt. Richie shouted, "We're sinking! I think this is quicksand!"

"Let's get out of here." I yelled and began to try to run back out of the mud flats. When it seemed like I was running in place and I started sinking, I stopped moving and looking back to see Richie was still way behind me.

The Deadly Mudflats of Cook Inlet, Anchorage Alaska

"Don't move;" I called to him. "It is like quicksand. You'll only make yourself sink more." The pull of the mud seemed to get stronger, but I decelerating and pulled slowly but as hard as I could, leaning forward and I kind of fell forward, but as my hands sank halfway up to my elbows, somehow my boots got free. I thought that if I could run on the top surface, but alter my weight from foot to foot so as not to put all my weight on each foot, the mud would not have time to suck me down. When I did get mostly up on top of the mud, I wanted to run, but instead I carefully shifted my weight and slowly walked out of the mud.

I looked back to see that Richie had stopped moving altogether, his boots now completely submerged in the mudflats.

"Help." Richie screamed. "I'm getting pulled into the quicksand."

I could see he was really scared. "Just lift up one foot at a time." I yelled. "Come on. You gotta be stronger than the mud to get out of there. Richie started crying and I didn't think he could hear me anyway, so I took a few steps backwards and cautiously stepped back onto the mudflat to help my brother. When I got there, just standing in place, I started to sink down into the mud. "Can you move at all?" I asked.

"No." Richie cried out, tears streaming from his eyes. "I can't move."

"Okay, okay." I said, trying to be calm as the mud had now engulfed my boots and I could feel myself still sinking. I reached down and pulled at one of Richie's legs. After a few tries, we were able to sloppily pull one of his feet loose. Richie's crying stopped as hope returned. The second leg was not as forgiving and seemed to be glued into the thick mud goop. "When I count to three," I said to Richie, "You need to put up at the same time I pull on your leg." This time with the combined effort, Richie's leg pulled free, but his right leg came out without his boot. Not waiting for me, Richie bolted one boot on one boot off, and ran all the way to the mudflat shore. Meanwhile by now, the mud had engulfed the hole where Richie's leg had been, leaving me to try to figure out where I needed to dig down to fish out his other boot.

While I continued moving ever-so-slightly in place so as not to sink any deeper, I was still slowly going descending. After sinking my hand down into the cold gray mud three or four times in the general area, I realized the boot may or may not be gone but if I didn't get out of there, I'd be lost. Using all the leg muscles I had, I pulled up and at the same time, Leaned over to one side. I could feel resistance of the mud wanted me and if not me, it wanted my boots too as a toll for my trespasses. Suddenly my left foot sloshed out with my boot on my foot, and even better, the motion seemed to loosen up the right side. As I lost my balance and fell forward, both hands into the mud, Richie loudly cried out, "Skipper, get out of there!"

I managed to get to my feet and then cautiously walked, slipping and sliding, but on top of the mud, to safe ground where Richie was.

"Let me catch my breath," I told Richie, as I was heaving for air. "I'll go back and get your other boot in a minute."

With a look of shock on Richie's face he said, "No. That's quicksand."

"What about your other boot?"

"I just want to go home." Richie cried. "Let's get out of here."

On the way back, we traded off wearing my right boot as Richie kept thanking me for saving his life, but with mud covering our hands and sleeves, and our brand-new raincoats now splattered everywhere with the gray matter, and mud painted all the way up to our knees, my thoughts were how much trouble we were going to be in when we got back home.

Fortune smiled on us that morning as we entered the trailer. Senior was gone and Grandpa Scarbrough was there to pick up the boys to take them fishing. Mother gasped at the sight of us and ushered us back outside where we took off all our clothes. We went back in and took a quick bath before getting fresh clothes on and recalling our misadventure to mother, John, David and Grandpa Scarbrough.

Before we finished telling our woeful tales, Richie started crying again. Grandpa Scarbrough turned to mother and said, "These boys are lucky to be alive, Eva. The mudflats can be as deep as eight feet. They can give way suddenly, and they can act like quicksand. " Grandpa squinted his eyes over at me when he continued, "The biggest problem with the mudflats is that most people don't know how to handle themselves if they get stuck." He looked over at David who seemed to think to was really funny. "The natural reaction is to scramble to try to free yourself," He looked back to mother, "The more you move around, the deeper you sink in."

Grandpa Scarbrough looked back at me when he said, "You boys are lucky the tide didn't come in. But Skip, that was real brave of you to go back and get Richie." Before I could bask in my wonderfulness, Grandpa Scarbrough said, "So, you guys ready to go fishing?"

Although mother put up a convincing argument why she and Richie and I should stay back, Grandpa Scarbrough insisted, and we all loaded up in his car for a good day fishing.

And you can see that Richie and I caught us some fine guppies while mother managed to get a fish almost as long as Richie himself.

As you can see Mother did much better than us

At first, Grandpa Scarbrough pretended to be angry with his daughter, seeing that mother caught a 38-pound salmon,... larger than any salmon he did, but then on the drive back, he couldn't stop admiring the trophy fish and complimenting mother.

When we got together with Senior that night, all the mud on our rain gear had been washed off, the clothes had already been laundered and nothing was said about our misadventures. But for years that followed, as Richie would recall the incident, I was always the hero that saved him from the quicksand. And it remained that way until the time we were climbing in the rock quarry in Iron Mountain where I was climbing above him and my footing accidentally rolled a rock (a sizable, 'larger than a softball' rock), down onto Richie's head. And when stories from the past come up, sadly, this is now what I'm remembered for, not, 'the quicksand rescuer and deliverer.'

Leave Well Enough Alone

(1986) – Love lost is a distressing and miserable thing, savior but a lost love being pursued anyway, for the sake of a reconciliation that will never happen, that is even more heartbreaking. This was a conceptual piece that took a hard right from what I had originally envisioned.

I had this idea, kind of like a music video, where I would be on a small stage in a small facility, maybe like a coffeehouse or small bar, where I have an audience in a, now long gone, smoke filled room. But I don't have their attention and they're all talking, interacting with each other, and maybe one or two of them glances up on the stage. And there I am on the stage singing my broken heart out to an audience that neither hears or comprehends the song. But nonetheless I continue singing about a long-lost love gone bad, and of an unpromising hope of reconciliation and renewed love.

Okay, that was kind of what I had in mind, but I only had four tracks and the sound effects of the bar or coffeehouse that I put at the beginning and end of this song were pretty much lost to the common listener. And unless you have headphones on and can listen real closely inside the rolling drums, just before the rest of the instruments break in; it doesn't exist. Also, I had a different lead guitar planned for the ending, but it didn't fit with the words and the forlorn harmonica music that I put in at the beginning and the end so I used a kind of steel guitar for a different effect and the organ background got changed too to be softer and supportive of the other guitar work.

Side Note:

Here again is a song that I really felt needed more attention and a redo, but that never happened. Well, that hasn't happened yet.

Call To Cause And Effect

(1991) – If we as citizens of the world loved our environment half as much as we should, there would be no need for this song. But between the argumentative posture of the bought-out-through-lobbyists republican direction and the indecisive wishy-washy democratic governance and poor stewardship control, we get what we voted for.

Still, sometimes I think most of us Americans are calloused by our surroundings; clean air, clean water, food in the stores, all to the point that we either don't think or want to think that there's a problem. And then there are those convinced that the scientists don't know what they're doing or maybe like the weatherman, is somehow winging it. Or maybe some of us feel that there isn't anything that can be done anyway, and we just let it go, hoping the course will right itself and the problem will eventually go away.

My friend Gary Rook, (Funeral Director – Forest Funeral Home), whose father owned and operated a used car lot in Ohio in the 50s and 60s, when speaking about older cars in general, once said, "You can take care of it now or you can take care of it later; but when you put things off, and take care of things later, it's always going to cost you more." And another saying he had, also about cars, "Abuse is second to neglect." Those prophetic sayings can be equated to a number of things; your older car, your teeth, your environment.

So, this song is a call to stop thinking in that manner and approach this from a different perspective; giving more consideration to what **you** can do to make this a better place to live in. Teach your children to be aware of their surroundings, to be of service to others, and that ***even one person*** can make a difference to a positive and hopeful tomorrow.

Side Note:

I'm pretty sure this is one of the longest songs to date but I wanted to have a thoughtful ending to march out of the song and the album. I really had fun doing this, but must say, the speed guitar chords took me a log time and a lot of takes to get it right.

I22

SOME PARTING
THOUGHTS

I may be repeating myself, and if so, please indulge me,... Here we have the third book (of four) that documents the memoirs and lyrics of the first 44 albums of Lord Baldwin, (Lord Chester L. Baldwin II).

These 44 albums, categorized as the *"Archive Series,"* were recorded during my, *"Analog"* era. The varied recordings were accomplished using one of the two TASCAM 4-track Cassette Recorders I used along the way,...

The body of work for, *'From The Lost Letters Sent - Book THREE'*

documents 79 songs and represents the recordings of the following ten albums of the Analog era;

* 21 – **That's America For You** *
* 22 – **One Step Closer To The Heart** *
* 23 – **Shifted Gears** *
* 24 – **New Suits** *
* 25 – **Listening To The News** *
* 26 – **Work** *
* 27 – **The New Lover's Waltz** *
* 28 – **On The Edge Of A Very Strange Light** *
* 29 – **Dreams For You** *
* 30 – **City Boy** *

These ten albums document the **Seventy-Nine** songs that were recorded between *July of 1993* and *April of 1994*,... This productivity was made possible partially by my taking the mandatory hour-long lunch period to write, every day,... the poetry (lyrics), sometimes writing two a day, but most of the time it would take me the whole hour or even two or three days to get it right,... And to be sure, maybe only one poem out of five was good enough to make the cut,... but that still meant about fifty a year might be considered,...Originally "Words For Songs" was going to be the title of this and the other books, but one night I was lying in bed trying to go to sleep and thinking I needed something else; something that could signify the state of affairs that is Lord Baldwin's music and the songs he writings. In 1989-1990 I started recording songs that I had written words for, or music I had composed and kept in my head since 1966.

When I created the first two albums and shared them with my family and friends, I was told that I should sell my cassettes to the music stores but I let them know that it was my hope and mission to create this portfolio of material, put music to the words, poems, lyrics, record the instruments, record my voice, engineer the production of the album, and then it is my mission to share that gift and talent with others. Yes, there always was that erstwhile element in the mix; the ego wants his genius to be known and compensated, but as that continued to never happen, to keep chasing the dream, there would have to be a different motivation. So, as I continued to give my work away, (since 1990), it was like a thank you to my Heavenly Father for the gifts and talents of music. But thinking spatially, I thought as how each one of my songs was kind of like a special letter, with its own individual message maybe making a statement before it is sent out there into the vastness of the universe, into space, a letter from me to you.

At a unique and particular occasion, each letter (song), with their time postmarked on the outside, would go out into the universe, maybe contemplating their hopes that the message would be received some-time, maybe not today, maybe not tomorrow, but someday. And these lost letters sent have been drifting in time and space for years, waiting, hoping for someone to find and open them, and read (hear), its mes-sage. And these lost letters are out there right now in the incalculable vastness of the cyber-digital cosmos, waiting to be discovered, calling out, "Come find me."

As I was originally putting this document together in 2001, as a project that I was doing at *The Evergreen State College*,... some of the stories and antidotes, fresh at the time, made a lot of sense, so I included them,... besides being fun diversions to the whole,... I believe the stories to be essential to help you gain a more balanced understand-ing,... and it was my hope that some of the stories could shed light on who I was, what I was doing, my motivations and what it was that shaped me to go in the directions I did and why I did not go in other directions when the opportunities presented themselves.

Regrettably, there is always so much more to include, but I needed to keep moving to get this work out and so, what you have here is not complete, nor do I think it ever will be. It is a work in progress though, and I reserve the right to revise, renew, renovate and or bring the "**Memoirs**" and "**Stories**" up to date.

Accepting the fact that the twelve percent accomplishments come at the time spent and expense cost of the eighty-eight practice writings that would eventually become, "just not good enough." Still, inside those twelve percent pieces some masterpieces have manifested themselves.

As Lord Baldwin's music is now streaming worldwide, this book may act as a companion guide for the listener of Lord Baldwin's material, and for those who might be interested in what thought-processes and insights that Lord Baldwin was going through or was influenced by, along with stories that may be related to the creative processes.

Lastly, I want to give thanks,…

I want to give thanks to the people and companies that without their product and services, I could not have presented such a package as you now have before you.

I am so thankful for the folks at **Yamaha** for creating and making the, **'PSR-500'** keyboard',… besides being so much fun and helping me delve into the magical and mystical realm of sounds and vibrations,… helping me to grow in as it stirred my imagination, encouraged a wild sense of inventiveness, demanding a sort of resourcefulness, and pushing my own envelope and creativity,…

I want to thank the folks that created, *Microsoft Office* for the tools they included in their software packages that allowed me to document and manipulate all of my *Microsoft Word* writings, my *Microsoft Excel* spreadsheets, my *Microsoft Access* databases and my *Microsoft Outlook* correspondences to put things together,.. also, all my finished album cover artwork was done with the sub-programs included in Microsoft Word, like *WordArt* and the, Pictures manipulation programs.

I want to thank the free, open-source, *GNU Image Manipulation Program, (GIMP 2.10.8)* of which I have come to love, although, I have barely scratched the surface of what this free, Adobe Photoshop - Photo & Design-like software can do, but it has saved me at least, $599.88 or the guilt I might have felt had I tried to pirate the Adobe software. Well done folks, well done indeed.

Big special thanks to my son *Brian's* best friend, (and my friend) *Jamie Stanger* who volunteered to work on my web page and was in the process of getting my web page, **(www.LordBaldwin.com)** up to date, in spite of the fact that he's fairly recently newly married to Jenna, they have a little 18-month-old boy, he got a new job and had to move near two hours away to be closer to his work. Still, this web page is very important to me as the possible face and liaisons to the *Lord Baldwin Happenings.* Jamie and Jenna continue to be inspirational and positive, with upbeat ideas and encouraging suggestions to make the Lord Baldwin web pages better.

I want to thank *Florian Heidenreich*, an Indie Software Developer living in Dresden with a background in professional software development for over twenty years, for his "**MP3TAG**" free software, of which I am so humbly grateful to for the digital tagging of all my Wav and MP3 files, (songs). Over the years I have come to think of Florian as a good friend who has been with me on my journey, helping me to accomplish great things through his simple but magnificent program. Again, well done indeed.

Thanks to the people at *"https://combinepdf.com/"* who's free online software helped me to manipulate and combine my varied PDF files. They also saved me from the guilt I would have felt, had I pirated that

Adobe software, also because of their free online service, I didn't have to pay $449.00 to the Adobe people for their Acrobat Pro software. Thank you, "CombinePDF.com."

I now wish to thank the very excellent people at *DistroKid* who helped me to get my music and song distributed and out throughout the world. I can't begin to express how grateful I am to finally have a chair to the world stage, and in spite of the number's rollercoaster of listeners, to have the ability to have people in Korea and Germany and India and Brazil and Norway and Japan and Australia and the United Kingdom be able to stream my material at any time and any place through Spotify and other streaming facilities is just so awesome. Thank you again folks so much for everything you've done for me. You guys rock!

As you can imagine, there are many other unsung heroes out there that I want to thank them for their help in making this new endeavor possible right now. And here is the shout out to *my lovely best friend, Diane* who unconditionally loves me and continues to believe in me, and inspires me to write the many love songs for her that she so richly and honorably deserves.

And here is my call out to *all my children and their children,...* Please know that I dedicate all of this thing I do to all of you and again, to **Diane**, with my most sincere love and devotion.

123

INDEX BY NAME OF SONG

Index by, 'Name of Song'
— Book THREE —

Other Books
BY
LORD CHESTER L. BALDWIN II

FROM THE LOST LETTERS SENT
Memoirs Of An Invisible Songwriter
Book ONE: 1985 – 1992

FROM THE LOST LETTERS SENT
Memoirs Of An Invisible Songwriter
Book TWO: 1992 – 1993

FROM THE LOST LETTERS SENT
Memoirs Of An Invisible Songwriter
Book THREE: 1993 – 1994

FROM THE LOST LETTERS SENT
Memoirs Of An Invisible Songwriter
Book FOUR: 1995 – 2001

STEPPING BETWEEN THE ANTS
Book ONE: *The Winter Escape*

STEPPING BETWEEN THE ANTS
Book TWO: *The Spring Ahead*

STEPPING BETWEEN THE ANTS
Book THREE: *A Summer To Remember*

STEPPING BETWEEN THE ANTS
Book FOUR: *The Fall Behind*

RESILIENT:
A (Web-Based Episodic) Musical Play & Story

'HEADS' or,
'TALES FROM THE SUMMER OF LOVE'